ASIAN COOKBOOK 2022

TRADITIONAL RECIPES EASY TO MAKE TO SURPRISE YOUR FAMILY AND FRIENDS

CHEN LIU

Table of Contents

Introduction *10*
   Chicken with Bamboo Shoots *11*
   Steamed Ham *12*
   Bacon with Cabbage *13*
   Almond Chicken *14*
   Chicken with Almonds and Water Chestnuts *16*
   Chicken with Almonds and Vegetables *17*
   Anise Chicken *18*
   Chicken with Apricots *20*
   Chicken with Asparagus *21*
   Chicken with Aubergine *22*
   Bacon-Wrapped Chicken *23*
   Chicken with Bean Sprouts *24*
   Chicken with Black Bean Sauce *25*
   Chicken with Broccoli *26*
   Chicken with Cabbage and Peanuts *27*
   Chicken with Cashews *28*
   Chicken with Chestnuts *30*
   Hot Chilli-Chicken *31*
   Stir-Fried Chicken with Chilli *32*
   Chicken Chop Suey *34*
   Chicken Chow Mein *35*
   Crispy-Fried Spiced Chicken *37*
   Fried Chicken with Cucumber *38*
   Chilli-Chicken Curry *40*
   Chinese Chicken Curry *41*
   Quick Curried Chicken *42*
   Curried Chicken with Potatoes *43*
   Deep-Fried Chicken Legs *44*
   Deep-Fried Chicken with Curry Sauce *45*
   Drunken Chicken *46*
   Savoury Chicken with Eggs *47*

Chicken Egg Rolls	49
Braised Chicken with Eggs	51
Far Eastern Chicken	53
Chicken Foo Yung	54
Ham and Chicken Foo Yung	55
Deep-Fried Chicken with Ginger	56
Ginger Chicken	57
Ginger Chicken with Mushrooms and Chestnuts	58
Golden Chicken	59
Marinated Golden Chicken Stew	60
Golden Coins	62
Steamed Chicken with Ham	63
Chicken with Hoisin Sauce	64
Honey Chicken	65
Kung Pao Chicken	66
Chicken with Leeks	67
Lemon Chicken	68
Lemon Chicken Stir-Fry	70
Chicken Livers with Bamboo Shoots	71
Deep-Fried Chicken Livers	72
Chicken Livers with Mangetout	73
Chicken Livers with Noodle Pancake	74
Chicken Livers with Oyster Sauce	75
Chicken Livers with Pineapple	76
Sweet and Sour Chicken Livers	77
Chicken with Lychees	78
Chicken with Lychee Sauce	79
Chicken with Mangetout	80
Chicken with Mangoes	81
Chicken-Stuffed Melon	82
Chicken and Mushroom Stir-Fry	83
Chicken with Mushrooms and Peanuts	84
Stir-Fried Chicken with Mushrooms	86
Steamed Chicken with Mushrooms	87
Chicken with Onions	88
Orange and Lemon Chicken	89

Chicken with Oyster Sauce	90
Chicken Parcels	91
Chicken with Peanuts	92
Chicken with Peanut Butter	93
Chicken with Peas	94
Peking Chicken	95
Chicken with Peppers	96
Stir-Fried Chicken with Peppers	98
Chicken and Pineapple	100
Chicken with Pineapple and Lychees	101
Chicken with Pork	102
Braised Chicken with Potatoes	103
Five-Spice Chicken with Potatoes	104
Red-Cooked Chicken	105
Chicken Rissoles	106
Savoury Chicken	107
Chicken in Sesame Oil	108
Sherry Chicken	109
Chicken with Soy Sauce	110
Spicy Baked Chicken	111
Chicken with Spinach	112
Chicken Spring Rolls	113
Simple Chicken Stir-Fry	115
Chicken in Tomato Sauce	116
Chicken with Tomatoes	117
Poached Chicken with Tomatoes	117
Chicken and Tomatoes with Black Bean Sauce	119
Quick-Cooked Chicken with Vegetables	120
Walnut Chicken	121
Chicken with Walnuts	122
Chicken with Water Chestnuts	123
Savoury Chicken with Water Chestnuts	124
Chicken Wontons	125
Crispy Chicken Wings	126
Five-Spice Chicken Wings	127
Marinated Chicken Wings	128

Royal Chicken Wings	130
Spiced Chicken Wings	131
Barbecued Chicken Drumsticks	132
Hoisin Chicken Drumsticks	133
Braised Chicken	134
Crispy-Fried Chicken	135
Deep-Fried Whole Chicken	136
Five-Spice Chicken	137
Ginger and Spring Onion Chicken	139
Poached Chicken	140
Red-Cooked Chicken	141
Red-Cooked Spiced Chicken	142
Sesame Roast Chicken	143
Chicken in Soy Sauce	144
Steamed Chicken	145
Steamed Chicken with Anise	146
Strange-Flavoured Chicken	147
Crispy Chicken Chunks	148
Chicken with Green Beans	149
Cooked Chicken with Pineapple	150
Chicken with Peppers and Tomatoes	151
Sesame Chicken	152
Fried Poussins	153
Turkey with Mangetout	154
Turkey with Peppers	156
Chinese Roast Turkey	158
Turkey with Walnuts and Mushrooms	159
Duck with Bamboo Shoots	160
Duck with Bean Sprouts	161
Braised Duck	162
Steamed Duck with Celery	163
Duck with Ginger	164
Duck with Green Beans	165
Deep-Fried Steamed Duck	166
Duck with Exotic Fruits	167
Braised Duck with Chinese Leaves	169

Drunken Duck	*170*
Five-Spice Duck	*171*
Stir-Fried Duck with Ginger	*172*
Duck with Ham and Leeks	*173*
Honey-Roast Duck	*174*
Moist Roast Duck	*175*
Stir-Fried Duck with Mushrooms	*176*
Duck with Two Mushrooms	*178*
Braised Duck with Onions	*179*
Duck with Orange	*181*
Orange-Roast Duck	*182*
Duck with Pears and Chestnuts	*183*
Peking Duck	*184*
Braised Duck with Pineapple	*186*
Stir-Fried Duck with Pineapple	*187*
Pineapple and Ginger Duck	*188*
Duck with Pineapple and Lychees	*189*
Duck with Pork and Chestnuts	*190*
Duck with Potatoes	*191*
Red-Cooked Duck	*193*
Rice Wine Roast Duck	*194*
Steamed Duck with Rice Wine	*195*
Savoury Duck	*196*
Savoury Duck with Green Beans	*197*
Slow-Cooked Duck	*198*
Stir-Fried Duck	*200*
Duck with Sweet Potatoes	*201*
Sweet and Sour Duck	*203*
Tangerine Duck	*204*
Duck with Vegetables	*205*
Stir-Fried Duck with Vegetables	*207*
White-Cooked Duck	*208*
Duck with Wine	*209*
Wine-Vapour Duck	*210*
Fried Pheasant	*211*
Pheasant with Almonds	*212*

Venison with Dried Mushrooms *213*
Salted Eggs *214*
Soy Eggs *215*
Tea Eggs *216*
Egg Custard *217*
Steamed Eggs *218*

Introduction

Everyone who loves to cook, loves to experiment with new dishes and new taste sensations. Asian cuisine has become immensely popular in recent years because it offers a different range of flavours to enjoy. Most dishes are cooked on top of the stove, and many are quickly prepared and cooked so are ideal for the busy cook who wants to create an appetising and attractive dish when there is little time to spare. If you really enjoy Far East cooking, you will probably already have a wok, and this is the perfect utensil for cooking most of the dishes in the book. If you have yet to be convinced that this style of cooking is for you, use a good frying pan or saucepan to try out the recipes. When you find how easy they are to prepare and how tasty to eat, you will almost certainly want to invest in a wok for your kitchen.

Chicken with Bamboo Shoots

Serves 4

45 ml/3 tbsp groundnut (peanut) oil
1 clove garlic, crushed
1 spring onion (scallion), chopped
1 slice ginger root, chopped
225 g/8 oz chicken breast, cut into slivers
225 g/8 oz bamboo shoots, cut into slivers
45 ml/3 tbsp soy sauce
15 ml/1 tbsp rice wine or dry sherry
5 ml/1 tsp cornflour (cornstarch)

Heat the oil and fry the garlic, spring onion and ginger until lightly browned. Add the chicken and stir-fry for 5 minutes. Add the bamboo shoots and stir-fry for 2 minutes. Stir in the soy sauce, wine or sherry and cornflour and stir-fry for about 3 minutes until the chicken is cooked through.

Steamed Ham

Serves 6–8

900 g/2 lb fresh ham

30 ml/2 tbsp brown sugar

60 ml/4 tbsp rice wine or dry sherry

Place the ham in a heatproof dish on a rack, cover and steam over boiling water for about 1 hour. Add the sugar and wine or sherry to the dish, cover and steam for a further 1 hour or until the ham is cooked. Leave to cool in the bowl before slicing.

Bacon with Cabbage

Serves 4

4 rashers streaky bacon, rinded and chopped
2.5 ml/½ tsp salt
1 slice ginger root, minced
½ cabbage, shredded
75 ml/5 tbsp chicken stock
15 ml/1 tbsp oyster sauce

Fry the bacon until crisp then remove it from the pan. Add the salt and ginger and stir-fry for 2 minutes. Add the cabbage and stir well then stir in the bacon and add the stock, cover and simmer for about 5 minutes until the cabbage is tender but still slightly crisp. Stir in the oyster sauce, cover and simmer for 1 minute before serving.

Almond Chicken

Serves 4–6

375 ml/13 fl oz/1½ cups chicken stock

60 ml/4 tbsp rice wine or dry sherry

45 ml/3 tbsp cornflour (cornstarch)

15 ml/1 tbsp soy sauce

4 chicken breasts

1 egg white

2.5 ml/½ tsp salt

oil for deep-frying

75 g/3 oz/½ cup blanched almonds

1 large carrot, diced

5 ml/1 tsp grated ginger root

6 spring onions (scallions), sliced

3 stalks celery, sliced

100 g/4 oz mushrooms, sliced

100 g/4 oz bamboo shoots, sliced

Mix the stock, half the wine or sherry, 30 ml/2 tbsp of cornflour, and the soy sauce in a saucepan. Bring to the boil, stirring, then simmer for 5 minutes until the mixture thickens. Remove from the heat and keep warm.

Remove the skin and bones from the chicken and cut it into 2.5 cm/1 in pieces. Mix the remaining wine or sherry and cornflour, the egg white and salt, add the chicken pieces and stir well. Heat the oil and fry the chicken pieces a few at a time for about 5 minutes until golden brown. Drain well. Remove all but 30 ml/ 2 tbsp of oil from the pan and stir-fry the almonds for 2 minutes until golden. Drain well. Add the carrot and ginger to the pan and stir-fry for 1 minute. Add the remaining vegetables and stir-fry for about 3 minutes until the vegetables are tender but still crisp. Return the chicken and almonds to the pan with the sauce and stir over a moderate heat for a few minutes until heated through.

Chicken with Almonds and Water Chestnuts

Serves 4

6 dried Chinese mushrooms

4 chicken pieces, boned

100 g/4 oz ground almonds

salt and freshly ground pepper

60 ml/4 tbsp groundnut (peanut) oil

100 g/4 oz water chestnuts, sliced

75 ml/5 tbsp chicken stock

30 ml/2 tbsp soy sauce

Soak the mushrooms in warm water for 30 minutes then drain. Discard the stalks and slice the caps. Thinly slice the chicken. Season the almonds generously with salt and pepper and coat the chicken slices in the almonds. Heat the oil and fry the chicken until lightly browned. Add the mushrooms, water chestnuts, stock and soy sauce, bring to the boil, cover and simmer for a few minutes until the chicken is cooked.

Chicken with Almonds and Vegetables

Serves 4

75 ml/5 tbsp groundnut (peanut) oil

4 slices ginger root, minced

5 ml/1 tsp salt

100 g/4 oz Chinese cabbage, shredded

50 g/2 oz bamboo shoots, diced

50 g/2 oz mushrooms, diced

2 stalks celery, diced

3 water chestnuts, diced

120 ml/4 fl oz/½ cup chicken stock

225 g/8 oz chicken breast, diced

15 ml/1 tbsp rice wine or dry sherry

50 g/2 oz mangetout (snow peas)

100 g/4 oz flaked almonds, toasted

10 ml/2 tsp cornflour (cornstarch)

15 ml/1 tbsp water

Heat half the oil and stir-fry the ginger and salt for 30 seconds. Add the cabbage, bamboo shoots, mushrooms, celery and water chestnuts and stir-fry for 2 minutes. Add the stock, bring to the boil, cover and simmer for 2 minutes. Remove the vegetables and sauce from the pan. Heat the remaining oil and fry the chicken for 1 minute. Add the wine or sherry and fry for 1 minute. Return the vegetables to the pan with the mangetout and almonds and simmer for 30 seconds. Blend the cornflour and water to a paste, stir it into the sauce and simmer, stirring, until the sauce thickens.

Anise Chicken

Serves 4

75 ml/5 tbsp groundnut (peanut) oil
2 onions, chopped
1 clove garlic, chopped
2 slices ginger root, chopped
15 ml/1 tbsp plain (all-purpose) flour
30 ml/2 tbsp curry powder
450 g/1 lb chicken, cubed
15 ml/1 tbsp sugar
30 ml/2 tbsp soy sauce
450 ml/¾ pt/2 cups chicken stock
2 cloves star anise
225 g/8 oz potatoes, diced

Heat half the oil and fry the onions until lightly browned then remove them from the pan. Heat the remaining oil and fry the garlic and ginger for 30 seconds. Stir in the flour and curry powder and cook for 2 minutes. Return the onions to the pan, add the chicken and stir-fry for 3 minutes. Add the sugar, soy sauce, stock and anise, bring to the boil, cover and simmer for 15 minutes. Add the potatoes, return to the boil, cover and simmer for a further 20 minutes until tender.

Chicken with Apricots

Serves 4

4 chicken pieces
salt and freshly ground pepper
pinch of ground ginger
60 ml/4 tbsp groundnut (peanut) oil
225 g/8 oz canned apricots, halved
300 ml/½ pt/1¼ cups Sweet and Sour Sauce
30 ml/2 tbsp flaked almonds, toasted

Season the chicken with salt, pepper and ginger. Heat the oil and fry the chicken until lightly browned. Cover and cook for about 20 minutes until tender, turning occasionally. Drain off the oil. Add the apricots and sauce to the pan, bring to the boil, cover and simmer gently for about 5 minutes or until heated through. Garnish with flaked almonds.

Chicken with Asparagus

Serves 4

45 ml/3 tbsp groundnut (peanut) oil

5 ml/1 tsp salt

1 clove garlic, crushed

1 spring onion (scallion), chopped

1 chicken breast, sliced

30 ml/2 tbsp black bean sauce

350 g/12 oz asparagus, cut into 2.5 cm/1 in pieces

120 ml/4 fl oz/½ cup chicken stock

5 ml/1 tsp sugar

15 ml/1 tbsp cornflour (cornstarch)

45 ml/3 tbsp water

Heat half the oil and fry the salt, garlic and spring onion until lightly browned. Add the chicken and fry until lightly coloured. Add the black bean sauce and stir to coat the chicken. Add the asparagus, stock and sugar, bring to the boil, cover and simmer for 5 minutes until the chicken is tender. Mix the cornflour and water to a paste, stir it into the pan and simmer, stirring, until the sauce clears and thickens.

Chicken with Aubergine

Serves 4

225 g/8 oz chicken, sliced
15 ml/1 tbsp soy sauce
15 ml/1 tbsp rice wine or dry sherry
15 ml/1 tbsp cornflour (cornstarch)
1 aubergine (eggplant), peeled and cut into strips
30 ml/2 tbsp groundnut (peanut) oil
2 dried red chilli peppers
2 cloves garlic, crushed
75 ml/5 tbsp chicken stock

Place the chicken in a bowl. Mix the soy sauce, wine or sherry and cornflour, stir into the chicken and leave to stand for 30 minutes. Blanch the aubergine in boiling water for 3 minutes then drain well. Heat the oil and fry the peppers until they darken then remove and discard them. Add the garlic and chicken and stir-fry until lightly coloured. Add the stock and aubergine, bring to the boil, cover and simmer for 3 minutes, stirring occasionally.

Bacon-Wrapped Chicken

Serves 4–6

225 g/8 oz chicken, cubed
30 ml/2 tbsp soy sauce
15 ml/1 tbsp rice wine or dry sherry
5 ml/1 tsp sugar
5 ml/1 tsp sesame oil
salt and freshly ground pepper
225 g/8 oz bacon rashers
1 eggs, lightly beaten
100 g/4 oz plain (all-purpose) flour
oil for deep-frying
4 tomatoes, sliced

Mix the chicken with the soy sauce, wine or sherry, sugar, sesame oil, salt and pepper. Cover and leave to marinate for 1 hour, stirring occasionally, then remove the chicken and discard the marinade. Cut the bacon into pieces and wrap it around the chicken cubes. Beat the eggs with the flour to make a thick batter, adding a little milk if necessary. Dip the cubes in the batter. Heat the oil and deep-fry the cubes until golden brown and cooked through. Serve garnished with tomatoes.

Chicken with Bean Sprouts

Serves 4

45 ml/3 tbsp groundnut (peanut) oil
1 clove garlic, crushed
1 spring onion (scallion), chopped
1 slice ginger root, chopped
225 g/8 oz chicken breast, cut into slivers
225 g/8 oz bean sprouts
45 ml/3 tbsp soy sauce
15 ml/1 tbsp rice wine or dry sherry
5 ml/1 tsp cornflour (cornstarch)

Heat the oil and fry the garlic, spring onion and ginger until lightly browned. Add the chicken and stir-fry for 5 minutes. Add the bean sprouts and stir-fry for 2 minutes. Stir in the soy sauce, wine or sherry and cornflour and stir-fry for about 3 minutes until the chicken is cooked through.

Chicken with Black Bean Sauce

Serves 4

30 ml/2 tbsp groundnut (peanut) oil

5 ml/1 tsp salt

30 ml/2 tbsp black bean sauce

2 cloves garlic, crushed

450 g/1 lb chicken, diced

250 ml/8 fl oz/1 cup stock

1 green pepper, diced

1 onion, chopped

15 ml/1 tbsp soy sauce

freshly ground pepper

15 ml/1 tbsp cornflour (cornstarch)

45 ml/3 tbsp water

Heat the oil and fry the salt, black beans and garlic for 30 seconds. Add the chicken and fry until lightly browned. Stir in the stock, bring to the boil, cover and simmer for 10 minutes. Add the pepper, onion, soy sauce and pepper, cover and simmer for a further 10 minutes. Blend the cornflour and water to a paste, stir into the sauce and simmer, stirring, until the sauce thickens and the chicken is tender.

Chicken with Broccoli

Serves 4

450 g/1 lb chicken meat, diced

225 g/8 oz chicken livers

45 ml/3 tbsp plain (all-purpose) flour

45 ml/3 tbsp groundnut (peanut) oil

1 onion, diced

1 red pepper, diced

1 green pepper, diced

225 g/8 oz broccoli florets

4 slices pineapple, diced

30 ml/2 tbsp tomato purée (paste)

30 ml/2 tbsp hoisin sauce

30 ml/2 tbsp honey

30 ml/2 tbsp soy sauce

300 ml/½ pt/1¼ cups chicken stock

10 ml/2 tsp sesame oil

Toss the chicken and chicken livers in the flour. Heat the oil and stir-fry the liver for 5 minutes then remove from the pan. Add the chicken, cover and fry over a moderate heat for 15 minutes, stirring occasionally. Add the vegetables and pineapple and stir-fry for 8 minutes. Return the livers to the wok, add the remaining ingredients and bring to the boil. Simmer, stirring, until the sauce thickens.

Chicken with Cabbage and Peanuts

Serves 4

45 ml/3 tbsp groundnut (peanut) oil
30 ml/2 tbsp peanuts
450 g/1 lb chicken, diced
½ cabbage, cut into squares
15 ml/1 tbsp black bean sauce
2 red chilli peppers, minced
5 ml/1 tsp salt

Heat a little oil and fry the peanuts for a few minutes, stirring continuously. Remove, drain then crush. Heat the remaining oil and fry the chicken and cabbage until lightly browned. Remove from the pan. Add the black bean sauce and chilli peppers and stir-fry for 2 minutes. Return the chicken and cabbage to the pan with the crushed peanuts and season with salt. Stir-fry until heated through then serve at once.

Chicken with Cashews

Serves 4

30 ml/2 tbsp soy sauce

30 ml/2 tbsp cornflour (cornstarch)

15 ml/1 tbsp rice wine or dry sherry

350 g/12 oz chicken, cubed

45 ml/3 tbsp groundnut (peanut) oil

2.5 ml/½ tsp salt

2 cloves garlic, crushed

225 g/8 oz mushrooms, sliced

100 g/4 oz water chestnuts, sliced

100 g/4 oz bamboo shoots

50 g/2 oz mangetout (snow peas)

225 g/8 oz/2 cups cashew nuts

300 ml/½ pt/1¼ cups chicken stock

Mix together the soy sauce, cornflour and wine or sherry, pour over the chicken, cover and leave to marinate for at least 1 hour. Heat 30 ml/2 tbsp of oil with the salt and garlic and fry until the garlic is lightly browned. Add the chicken with the marinade and stir-fry for 2 minutes until the chicken is lightly browned. Add the mushrooms, water chestnuts, bamboo shoots and mangetout and stir-fry for 2 minutes. Meanwhile, heat the remaining oil in a separate pan and fry the cashew nuts over a gentle heat for a few minutes until golden brown. Add them to the pan with the stock, bring to the boil, cover and simmer for 5 minutes. If the sauce has not thickened sufficiently, stir in a little cornflour blended with a spoonful of water and stir until the sauce thickens and clears.

Chicken with Chestnuts

Serves 4

225 g/8 oz chicken, sliced

5 ml/1 tsp salt

15 ml/1 tbsp soy sauce

oil for deep-frying

250 ml/8 fl oz/1 cup chicken stock

200 g/7 oz water chestnuts, chopped

225 g/8 oz chestnuts, chopped

225 g/8 oz mushrooms, quartered

15 ml/1 tbsp chopped fresh parsley

Sprinkle the chicken with salt and soy sauce and rub it well into the chicken. Heat the oil and deep-fry the chicken until golden brown then remove and drain. Place the chicken in a pan with the stock, bring to the boil and simmer for 5 minutes. Add the water chestnuts, chestnuts and mushrooms, cover and simmer for about 20 minutes until everything is tender. Serve garnished with parsley.

Hot Chilli-Chicken

Serves 4

350 g/1 lb chicken meat, cubed
1 egg, lightly beaten
10 ml/2 tsp soy sauce
2.5 ml/½ tsp cornflour (cornstarch)
oil for deep-frying
1 green pepper, diced
4 cloves garlic, crushed
2 red chilli peppers, shredded
5 ml/1 tsp freshly ground pepper
5 ml/1 tsp wine vinegar
5 ml/1 tsp water
2.5 ml/½ tsp sugar
2.5 ml/½ tsp chilli oil
2.5 ml/½ tsp sesame oil

Mix the chicken with the egg, half the soy sauce and the cornflour and leave to stand for 30 minutes. Heat the oil and deep-fry the chicken until golden brown then drain well. Pour off all but 15 ml/1 tbsp of oil from the pan, add the pepper, garlic and chilli peppers and fry for 30 seconds. Add the pepper, wine vinegar, water and sugar and fry for 30 seconds. Return the chicken to the pan and stir-fry for a few minutes until cooked through. Serve sprinkled with chilli and sesame oils.

Stir-Fried Chicken with Chilli

Serves 4

225 g/8 oz chicken, sliced

2.5 ml/½ tsp soy sauce

2.5 ml/½ tsp sesame oil

2.5 ml/½ tsp rice wine or dry sherry

5 ml/1 tsp cornflour (cornstarch)

salt

45 ml/3 tbsp groundnut (peanut) oil

100 g/4 oz spinach

4 spring onions (scallions), chopped

2.5 ml/½ tsp chilli powder

15 ml/1 tbsp water

1 tomato, sliced

Mix the chicken with the soy sauce, sesame oil, wine or sherry, half the cornflour and a pinch of salt. Leave to stand for 30 minutes. Heat 15 ml/ 1 tbsp of oil and fry the chicken until lightly browned. Remove from the wok. Heat 15 ml/1 tbsp of oil and stir-fry the spinach until wilted then remove it from the wok. Heat the remaining oil and fry the spring onions, chilli powder, water and remaining cornflour for 2 minutes. Stir in the chicken and stir-fry quickly. Arrange the spinach around a warmed serving plate, top with the chicken and serve garnished with tomatoes.

Chicken Chop Suey

Serves 4

100 g/4 oz Chinese leaves, shredded

100 g/4 oz bamboo shoots, cut into strips

60 ml/4 tbsp groundnut (peanut) oil

3 spring onions (scallions), sliced

2 cloves garlic, crushed

1 slice ginger root, chopped

225 g/8 oz chicken breast, cut into strips

45 ml/3 tbsp soy sauce

15 ml/1 tbsp rice wine or dry sherry

5 ml/1 tsp salt

2.5 ml/½ tsp sugar

freshly ground pepper

15 ml/1 tbsp cornflour (cornstarch)

Blanch the Chinese leaves and bamboo shoots in boiling water for 2 minutes. Drain and pat dry. Heat 45 ml/3 tbsp of oil and fry the onions, garlic and ginger until lightly browned. Add the chicken and stir-fry for 4 minutes. Remove from the pan. Heat the remaining oil and stir-fry the vegetables for 3 minutes. Add the chicken, soy sauce, wine or sherry, salt, sugar and a pinch of pepper and stir-fry for 1 minute. Mix the cornflour with a little water, stir it into the sauce and simmer, stirring, until the sauce clears and thickens.

Chicken Chow Mein

Serves 4

30 ml/2 tbsp groundnut (peanut) oil
2 cloves garlic, crushed
450 g/1 lb chicken, sliced
225 g/8 oz bamboo shoots, sliced
100 g/4 oz celery, sliced
225 g/8 oz mushrooms, sliced
450 ml/¾ pt/2 cups chicken stock
225 g/8 oz bean sprouts
4 onions, cut into wedges
30 ml/2 tbsp soy sauce
30 ml/2 tbsp cornflour (cornstarch)
225 g/8 oz dried Chinese noodles

Heat the oil with the garlic until lightly golden then add the chicken and stir-fry for 2 minutes until lightly browned. Add the bamboo shoots, celery and mushrooms and stir-fry for 3 minutes. Add most of the stock, bring to the boil, cover and simmer for 8 minutes. Add the bean sprouts and onions and simmer for 2 minutes, stirring, until there is just a little stock remaining. Mix together the remaining stock with the soy sauce and cornflour. Stir it into the pan and simmer, stirring, until the sauce clears and thickens.

Meanwhile, cook the noodles in boiling salted water for a few minutes, according to the instructions on the packet. Drain well then toss with the chicken mixture and serve at once.

Crispy-Fried Spiced Chicken

Serves 4

450 g/1 lb chicken meat, cut into chunks

30 ml/2 tbsp soy sauce

30 ml/2 tbsp plum sauce

45 ml/3 tbsp mango chutney

1 clove garlic, crushed

2.5 ml/½ tsp ground ginger

few drops of brandy

30 ml/2 tbsp cornflour (cornstarch)

2 eggs, beaten

100 g/4 oz/1 cup dried breadcrumbs

30 ml/2 tbsp groundnut (peanut) oil

6 spring onions (scallions), chopped

1 red pepper, diced

1 green pepper, diced

30 ml/2 tbsp soy sauce

30 ml/2 tbsp honey

30 ml/2 tbsp wine vinegar

Place the chicken in a bowl. Mix the sauces, chutney, garlic, ginger and brandy, pour over the chicken, cover and leave to marinate for 2 hours. Drain the chicken then dust it with cornflour. Coat in eggs then breadcrumbs. Heat the oil then fry the chicken until golden brown. Remove from the pan. Add the vegetables and stir-fry for 4 minutes then remove. Drain the oil from the pan then return the chicken and vegetables to the pan with the remaining ingredients. Bring to the boil and heat through before serving.

Fried Chicken with Cucumber

Serves 4

225 g/8 oz chicken meat

1 egg white

2.5 ml/½ tsp cornflour (cornstarch)

salt

½ cucumber

30 ml/2 tbsp groundnut (peanut) oil

100 g/4 oz button mushrooms

50 g/2 oz bamboo shoots, cut into strips

50 g/2 oz ham, diced

15 ml/1 tbsp water

2.5 ml/½ tsp salt

2.5 ml/½ tsp rice wine or dry sherry

2.5 ml/½ tsp sesame oil

Slice the chicken and cut it into chunks. Mix with the egg white, cornflour and salt and leave to stand. Halve the cucumber lengthways and cut diagonally into thick slices. Heat the oil and stir-fry the chicken until lightly browned then remove from the pan. Add the cucumber and bamboo shoots and stir-fry for 1 minute. Return the chicken to the pan with the ham, water, salt and wine or sherry. Bring to the boil and simmer until the chicken is tender. Serve sprinkled with sesame oil.

Chilli-Chicken Curry

Serves 4

120 ml/4 fl oz/½ cup groundnut (peanut) oil
4 chicken pieces
1 onion, chopped
5 ml/1 tsp curry powder
5 ml/1 tsp chilli sauce
15 ml/1 tbsp rice wine or dry sherry
2.5 ml/½ tsp salt
600 ml/1 pt/2½ cups chicken stock
15 ml/1 tbsp cornflour (cornstarch)
45 ml/3 tbsp water
5 ml/1 tsp sesame oil

Heat the oil and fry the chicken pieces until golden brown on both sides then remove them from the pan. Add the onion, curry powder and chilli sauce and stir-fry for 1 minute. Add the wine or sherry and salt, stir well, then return the chicken to the pan and stir again. Add the stock, bring to the boil and simmer gently for about 30 minutes until the chicken is tender. If the sauce has not reduced sufficiently, blend the cornflour and water to a paste, stir a little into the sauce and simmer, stirring, until the sauce thickens. Serve sprinkled with sesame oil.

Chinese Chicken Curry

Serves 4

45 ml/3 tbsp curry powder

1 onion, sliced

350 g/12 oz chicken, diced

150 ml/¼ pt/generous ½ cup chicken stock

5 ml/1 tsp salt

10 ml/2 tsp cornflour (cornstarch)

15 ml/1 tbsp water

Heat the curry powder and onion in a dry pan for 2 minutes, shaking the pan to coat the onion. Add the chicken and stir until well coated in curry powder. Add the stock and salt, bring to the boil, cover and simmer for about 5 minutes until the chicken is tender. Mix the cornflour and water to a paste, stir into the pan and simmer, stirring, until the sauce thickens.

Quick Curried Chicken

Serves 4

450 g/1 lb chicken breasts, cubed

45 ml/3 tbsp rice wine or dry sherry

50 g/2 oz cornflour (cornstarch)

1 egg white

salt

150 ml/¼ pt/generous ½ cup groundnut (peanut) oil

15 ml/1 tbsp curry powder

10 ml/2 tsp brown sugar

150 ml/¼ pt/generous ½ cup chicken stock

Mix together the chicken cubes and sherry. Reserve 10 ml/2 tsp of the cornflour. Beat the egg white with the remaining cornflour and a pinch of salt then stir it into the chicken until it is well coated. Heat the oil and fry the chicken until cooked and golden. Remove from the pan and drain off all but 15 ml/1 tbsp of the oil. Stir in the reserved cornflour, curry powder and sugar and fry for 1 minute. Stir in the stock, bring to the boil and simmer, stirring continuously, until the sauce thickens. Return the chicken to the pan, stir together and reheat before serving.

Curried Chicken with Potatoes

Serves 4

45 ml/3 tbsp groundnut (peanut) oil

2.5 ml/½ tsp salt

1 clove garlic, crushed

750 g/1½ lb chicken, cubed

225 g/8 oz potatoes, cubed

4 onions, cut into wedges

15 ml/1 tbsp curry powder

450 ml/¾ pt/2 cups chicken stock

225 g/8 oz mushrooms, sliced

Heat the oil with the salt and garlic, add the chicken and fry until lightly browned. Add the potatoes, onions and curry powder and stir-fry for 2 minutes. Add the stock, bring to the boil, cover and simmer for about 20 minutes until the chicken is cooked, stirring occasionally. Add the mushrooms, remove the lid and simmer for a further 10 minutes until the liquid has reduced.

Deep-Fried Chicken Legs

Serves 4

2 large chicken legs, boned
2 spring onions (scallions)
1 slice ginger, beaten flat
120 ml/4 fl oz/½ cup soy sauce
5 ml/1 tsp rice wine or dry sherry
oil for deep-frying
5 ml/1 tsp sesame oil
freshly ground pepper

Spread out the chicken flesh and score it all over. Beat 1 spring onion flat and chop the other. Mix tine flattened spring onion with the ginger, soy sauce and wine or sherry. Pour over the chicken and leave to marinate for 30 minutes. Remove and drain. Place on a plate on a steamer rack and steam for 20 minutes.

Heat the oil and deep-fry the chicken for about 5 minutes until golden brown. Remove from the pan, drain well and slice thickly, then arrange the slices on a warmed serving plate. Heat the sesame oil, add the chopped spring onion and pepper, pour over the chicken and serve.

Deep-Fried Chicken with Curry Sauce

Serves 4

1 egg, lightly beaten

30 ml/2 tbsp cornflour (cornstarch)

25 g/1 oz/¼ cup plain (all-purpose) flour

2.5 ml/½ tsp salt

225 g/8 oz chicken, cubed

oil for deep-frying

30 ml/2 tbsp groundnut (peanut) oil

30 ml/2 tbsp curry powder

60 ml/4 tbsp rice wine or dry sherry

Beat the egg with the cornflour, flour and salt to a thick batter. Pour over the chicken and stir well to coat. Heat the oil and deep-fry the chicken until golden brown and cooked through. Meanwhile, heat the oil and fry the curry powder for 1 minute. Stir in the wine or sherry and bring to the boil. Place the chicken on a warmed plate and pour over the curry sauce.

Drunken Chicken

Serves 4

450 g/1 lb chicken fillet, cut into chunks
60 ml/4 tbsp soy sauce
30 ml/2 tbsp hoisin sauce
30 ml/2 tbsp plum sauce
30 ml/2 tbsp wine vinegar
2 cloves garlic, crushed
pinch of salt
few drops of chilli oil
2 egg whites
60 ml/4 tbsp cornflour (cornstarch)
oil for deep-frying
200 ml/½ pt/1¼ cups rice wine or dry sherry

Place the chicken in a bowl. Mix the sauces and wine vinegar, garlic, salt and chilli oil, pour over the chicken and marinate in the refrigerator for 4 hours. Beat the egg whites until stiff and fold in the cornflour. Remove the chicken from the marinade and coat with the egg white mixture. Heat the oil and deep-fry the chicken until cooked through and golden brown. Drain well on kitchen paper and place in a bowl. Pour over the wine or sherry, cover and leave to marinate in the refrigerator for 12 hours. Remove the chicken from the wine and serve cold.

Savoury Chicken with Eggs

Serves 4

30 ml/2 tbsp groundnut (peanut) oil
4 chicken pieces
2 spring onions (scallions), chopped
1 clove garlic, crushed
1 slice ginger root, chopped
175 ml/6 fl oz/¾ cup soy sauce
30 ml/2 tbsp rice wine or dry sherry
30 ml/2 tbsp brown sugar
5 ml/1 tsp salt
375 ml/13 fl oz/1½ cups water
4 hard-boiled (hard-cooked) eggs
15 ml/1 tbsp cornflour (cornstarch)

Heat the oil and fry the chicken pieces until golden brown. Add the spring onions, garlic and ginger and fry for 2 minutes. Add the soy sauce, wine or sherry, sugar and salt and stir together well. Add the water and bring to the boil, cover and simmer for 20 minutes. Add the hard-boiled eggs, cover and cook for a further 15 minutes. Mix the cornflour with a little water, stir it into the sauce and simmer, stirring, until the sauce clears and thickens.

Chicken Egg Rolls

Serves 4

4 dried Chinese mushrooms
100 g/4 oz chicken, cut into strips
5 ml/1 tsp cornflour (cornstarch)
15 ml/1 tbsp soy sauce
2.5 ml/½ tsp salt
2.5 ml/½ tsp sugar
60 ml/4 tbsp groundnut (peanut) oil
225 g/8 oz bean sprouts
3 spring onions (scallions), chopped
100 g/4 oz spinach
12 egg roll skins
1 egg, beaten
oil for deep-frying

Soak the mushrooms in warm water for 30 minutes then drain. Discard the stalks and chop the caps. Place the chicken in a bowl. Mix the cornflour with 5 ml/1 tsp of soy sauce, the salt and sugar and stir into the chicken. Leave to stand for 15 minutes. Heat half the oil and stir-fry the chicken until lightly browned. Blanch the bean sprouts in boiling water for 3 minutes then drain. Heat the remaining oil and fry the spring onions until lightly browned. Stir in the mushrooms, bean sprouts, spinach and remaining soy sauce. Add in the chicken and stir-fry for 2 minutes. Leave to cool. Place a little filling on the centre of each skin and brush the edges with beaten egg. Fold in the sides then roll up the egg rolls, sealing the edges with egg. Heat the oil and deep-fry the egg rolls until crisp and golden.

Braised Chicken with Eggs

Serves 4

30 ml/2 tbsp groundnut (peanut) oil
4 chicken breast fillets, cut into strips
1 red pepper, cut into strips
1 green pepper, cut into strips
45 ml/3 tbsp soy sauce
45 ml/3 tbsp rice wine or dry sherry
250 ml/8 fl oz/1 cup chicken stock
100 g/4 oz iceberg lettuce, shredded
5 ml/1 tsp brown sugar
30 ml/2 tbsp hoisin sauce
salt and pepper
15 ml/1 tbsp cornflour (cornstarch)
30 ml/2 tbsp water
4 eggs
30 ml/2 tbsp sherry

Heat the oil and fry the chicken and peppers until golden brown. Add the soy sauce, wine or sherry and stock, bring to the boil, cover and simmer for 30 minutes. Add the lettuce, sugar and hoisin sauce and season with salt and pepper. Mix the cornflour and water, stir it into the sauce and bring to the boil, stirring.

Beat the eggs with the sherry and fry as thin omelettes. Sprinkle with salt and pepper and tear into strips. Arrange in a warmed serving dish and spoon over the chicken.

Far Eastern Chicken

Serves 4

60 ml/4 tbsp groundnut (peanut) oil
450 g/1 lb chicken meat, cut into chunks
2 cloves garlic, crushed
2.5 ml/½ tsp salt
2 onions, chopped
2 pieces stem ginger, chopped
45 ml/3 tbsp soy sauce
30 ml/2 tbsp hoisin sauce
45 ml/3 tbsp rice wine or dry sherry
300 ml/½ pt/1¼ cups chicken stock
5 ml/1 tsp freshly ground pepper
6 hard-boiled (hard-cooked) eggs, chopped
15 ml/1 tbsp cornflour (cornstarch)
15 ml/1 tbsp water

Heat the oil and fry the chicken until golden brown. Add the garlic, salt, onions and ginger and fry for 2 minutes. Add the soy sauce, hoisin sauce, wine or sherry, stock and pepper. Bring to the boil, cover and simmer for 30 minutes. Add the eggs. Mix the cornflour and water and stir it into the sauce. Bring to the boil and simmer, stirring, until the sauce thickens.

Chicken Foo Yung

Serves 4

6 eggs, beaten

45 ml/3 tbsp cornflour (cornstarch)

100 g/4 oz mushrooms, roughly chopped

225 g/8 oz chicken breast, diced

1 onion, finely chopped

5 ml/1 tsp salt

45 ml/3 tbsp groundnut (peanut) oil

Beat the eggs then beat in the cornflour. Stir in all the remaining ingredients except the oil. Heat the oil. Pour the mixture into the pan a little at a time to make small pancakes about 7.5 cm/3 in across. Cook until the bottom is golden brown then turn and cook the other side.

Ham and Chicken Foo Yung

Serves 4

6 eggs, beaten

45 ml/3 tbsp cornflour (cornstarch)

100 g/4 oz ham, diced

225 g/8 oz chicken breast, diced

3 spring onions (scallions), finely chopped

5 ml/1 tsp salt

45 ml/3 tbsp groundnut (peanut) oil

Beat the eggs then beat in the cornflour. Stir in all the remaining ingredients except the oil. Heat the oil. Pour the mixture into the pan a little at a time to make small pancakes about 7.5 cm/3 in across. Cook until the bottom is golden brown then turn and cook the other side.

Deep-Fried Chicken with Ginger

Serves 4

1 chicken, halved

4 slices ginger root, crushed

30 ml/2 tbsp rice wine or dry sherry

30 ml/2 tbsp soy sauce

5 ml/1 tsp sugar

oil for deep-frying

Place the chicken in a shallow bowl. Mix the ginger, wine or sherry, soy sauce and sugar, pour over the chicken and rub into the skin. Leave to marinate for 1 hour. Heat the oil and deep-fry the chicken, one half at a time, until lightly coloured. Remove from the oil and leave to cool slightly while you reheat the oil. Return the chicken to the pan and deep-fry until golden brown and cooked through. Drain well before serving.

Ginger Chicken

Serves 4

225 g/8 oz chicken, thinly sliced

1 egg white

pinch of salt

2.5 ml/½ tsp cornflour (cornstarch)

15 ml/1 tbsp groundnut (peanut) oil

10 slices ginger root

6 mushrooms, halved

1 carrot, sliced

2 spring onions (scallions), sliced

5 ml/1 tsp rice wine or dry sherry

5 ml/1 tsp water

2.5 ml/½ tsp sesame oil

Mix the chicken with the egg white, salt and cornflour. Heat half the oil and fry the chicken until lightly browned then remove it from the pan. Heat the remaining oil and fry the ginger, mushrooms, carrot and spring onions for 3 minutes. Return the chicken to the pan with the wine or sherry and water and simmer until the chicken is tender. Serve sprinkled with sesame oil.

Ginger Chicken with Mushrooms and Chestnuts

Serves 4

60 ml/4 tbsp groundnut (peanut) oil
225 g/8 oz onions, sliced
450 g/1 lb chicken meat, diced
100 g/4 oz mushrooms, sliced
30 ml/2 tbsp plain (all-purpose) flour
60 ml/4 tbsp soy sauce
10 ml/2 tsp sugar
salt and freshly ground pepper
900 ml/1½ pt/3¾ cups hot water
2 slices ginger root, chopped
450 g/1 lb water chestnuts

Heat the half oil and fry the onions for 3 minutes then remove them from the pan. Heat the remaining oil and fry the chicken until lightly browned.

Add the mushrooms and cook for 2 minutes. Sprinkle the mixture with flour then stir in the soy sauce, sugar, salt and pepper. Pour in the water and ginger, onions and chestnuts. Bring to the boil, cover and simmer gently for 20 minutes. Remove the lid and continue to simmer gently until the sauce has reduced.

Golden Chicken

Serves 4

8 small chicken pieces
300 ml/½ pt/1¼ cups chicken stock
45 ml/3 tbsp soy sauce
15 ml/1 tbsp rice wine or dry sherry
5 ml/1 tsp sugar
1 sliced ginger root, minced

Place all the ingredients in a large pan, bring to the boil, cover and simmer for about 30 minutes until the chicken is thoroughly cooked. Remove the lid and continue to simmer until the sauce has reduced.

Marinated Golden Chicken Stew

Serves 4

4 chicken pieces

300 ml/½ pt/1¼ cups soy sauce

oil for deep-frying

4 spring onions (scallions), thickly sliced

1 slice ginger root, minced

2 red chilli peppers, sliced

3 cloves star anise

50 g/2 oz bamboo shoots, sliced

150 ml/1½ pt/generous ½ cup chicken stock

30 ml/2 tbsp cornflour (cornstarch)

60 ml/4 tbsp water

5 ml/1 tsp sesame oil

Cut the chicken into large chunks and marinate in the soy sauce for 10 minutes. Remove and drain, reserving the soy sauce. Heat the oil and deep-fry the chicken for about 2 minutes until lightly browned. Remove and drain. Pour off all but 30 ml/2 tbsp of the oil then add the spring onions, ginger, chilli peppers and star anise and fry for 1 minute. Return the chicken to the pan with the bamboo shoots and reserved soy sauce and add just enough stock to cover the chicken. Bring to the boil and simmer for about 10 minutes until the chicken is tender. Remove the chicken from the sauce with a slotted spoon and arrange on a warmed serving dish. Strain the sauce then return it to the pan. Blend the cornflour and water to a paste, stir into the sauce and simmer, stirring, until the sauce thickens. Pour over the chicken and serve sprinkled with a little sesame oil.

Golden Coins

Serves 4

4 chicken breast fillets

30 ml/2 tbsp honey

30 ml/2 tbsp wine vinegar

30 ml/2 tbsp tomato ketchup (catsup)

30 ml/2 tbsp soy sauce

pinch of salt

2 cloves garlic, crushed

5 ml/1 tsp five-spice powder

45 ml/3 tbsp plain (all-purpose) flour

2 eggs, beaten

5 ml/1 tsp grated root ginger

5 ml/1 tsp grated lemon rind

100 g/4 oz/1 cup dried breadcrumbs

oil for deep-frying

Put the chicken into a bowl. Mix together the honey, wine vinegar, tomato ketchup, soy sauce, salt, garlic and five-spice powder. Pour over the chicken, stir well, cover and marinate in the refrigerator for 12 hours.

Remove the chicken from the marinade and cut into finger thick strips. Dust with flour. Beat the eggs, ginger and lemon rind.

Coat the chicken in the mixture then in the breadcrumbs until evenly coated. Heat the oil and deep-fry the chicken until golden brown.

Steamed Chicken with Ham

Serves 4

4 chicken portions
100 g/4 oz smoked ham, chopped
3 spring onions (scallions), chopped
15 ml/1 tbsp groundnut (peanut) oil
salt and freshly ground pepper
15 ml/1 tbsp flat-leaved parsley

Chop the chicken portions into 5 cm/1 in chunks and place in an ovenproof bowl with the ham and spring onions. Sprinkle with oil and season with salt and pepper then toss the ingredients together gently. Place the bowl on a rack in a steamer, cover and steam over boiling water for about 40 minutes until the chicken is tender. Serve garnished with parsley.

Chicken with Hoisin Sauce

Serves 4

4 chicken portions, halved
50 g/2 oz/½ cup cornflour (cornstarch)
oil for deep-frying
10 ml/2 tsp grated ginger root
2 onions, chopped
225 g/8 oz broccoli florets
1 red pepper, chopped
225 g/8 oz button mushrooms
250 ml/8 fl oz/1 cup chicken stock
45 ml/3 tbsp rice wine or dry sherry
45 ml/3 tbsp cider vinegar
45 ml/3 tbsp hoisin sauce
20 ml/4 tsp soy sauce

Coat the chicken pieces in half the cornflour. Heat the oil and fry the chicken pieces a few at a time for about 8 minutes until golden brown and cooked through. Remove from the pan and drain on kitchen paper. Remove all but 30 ml/2 tbsp of oil from the pan and stir-fry the ginger for 1 minute. Add the onions and stir-fry for 1 minute. Add the broccoli, pepper and mushrooms and stir-fry for 2 minutes. Combine the stock with the reserved cornflour and remaining ingredients and add to the pan. Bring to the boil, stirring, and cook until the sauce clears. Return the chicken to the wok and cook, stirring, for about 3 minutes until heated through.

Honey Chicken

Serves 4

30 ml/2 tbsp groundnut (peanut) oil
4 chicken pieces
30 ml/2 tbsp soy sauce
120 ml/4 fl oz/½ cup rice wine or dry sherry
30 ml/2 tbsp honey
5 ml/1 tsp salt
1 spring onion (scallion), chopped
1 slice ginger root, finely chopped

Heat the oil and fry the chicken until browned on all sides. Drain off excess oil. Mix together the remaining ingredients and pour them into the pan. Bring to the boil, cover and simmer for about 40 minutes until the chicken is cooked through.

Kung Pao Chicken

Serves 4

450 g/1 lb chicken, cubed
1 egg white
5 ml/1 tsp salt
30 ml/2 tbsp cornflour (cornstarch)
60 ml/4 tbsp groundnut (peanut) oil
25 g/1 oz dried red chilli peppers, trimmed
5 ml/1 tsp minced garlic
15 ml/1 tbsp soy sauce
15 ml/1 tbsp rice wine or dry sherry 5 ml/1 tsp sugar
5 ml/1 tsp wine vinegar
5 ml/1 tsp sesame oil
30 ml/2 tbsp water

Place the chicken in a bowl with the egg white, salt and half the cornflour and leave to marinate for 30 minutes. Heat the oil and fry the chicken until lightly browned then remove it from the pan. Reheat the oil and fry the chilli peppers and garlic for 2 minutes. Return the chicken to the pan with the soy sauce, wine or sherry, sugar, wine vinegar and sesame oil and stir-fry for 2 minutes. Mix the remaining cornflour with the water, stir it into the pan and simmer, stirring, until the sauce clears and thickens.

Chicken with Leeks

Serves 4

30 ml/2 tbsp groundnut (peanut) oil

5 ml/1 tsp salt

225 g/8 oz leeks, sliced

1 slice ginger root, chopped

225 g/8 oz chicken, thinly sliced

15 ml/1 tbsp rice wine or dry sherry

15 ml/1 tbsp soy sauce

Heat half the oil and fry the salt and leeks until lightly browned then remove them from the pan. Heat the remaining oil and fry the ginger and chicken until lightly browned. Add the wine or sherry and soy sauce and fry for a further 2 minutes until the chicken is cooked. Return the leeks to the pan and stir together until heated through. Serve at once.

Lemon Chicken

Serves 4

4 boned chicken breasts

2 eggs

50 g/2 oz/½ cup cornflour (cornstarch)

50 g/2 oz/½ cup plain (all-purpose) flour

150 ml/¼ pt/generous ½ cup water

groundnut (peanut) oil for deep-frying

250 ml/8 fl oz/1 cup chicken stock

60 ml/5 tbsp lemon juice

30 ml/2 tbsp rice wine or dry sherry

30 ml/2 tbsp cornflour (cornstarch)

30 ml/2 tbsp tomato purée (paste)

1 head lettuce

Cut each chicken breast into 4 pieces. Beat the eggs, cornflour and plain flour, adding just enough water to make a thick batter. Place the chicken pieces in the batter and stir until thoroughly coated. Heat the oil and deep-fry the chicken until golden brown and cooked through.

Meanwhile, mix the stock, lemon juice, wine or sherry, cornflour and tomato purée and heat gently, stirring, until the mixture comes to the boil. Simmer gently, stirring continuously, until the sauce thickens and clears. Arrange the chicken on a warmed serving plate on a bed of lettuce leaves and either pour over the sauce or serve it separately.

Lemon Chicken Stir-Fry

Serves 4

450 g/1 lb boned chicken, sliced
30 ml/2 tbsp lemon juice
15 ml/1 tbsp soy sauce
15 ml/1 tbsp rice wine or dry sherry
30 ml/2 tbsp cornflour (cornstarch)
30 ml/2 tbsp groundnut (peanut) oil
2.5 ml/½ tsp salt
2 cloves garlic, crushed
50 g/2 oz water chestnuts, cut into strips
50 g/2 oz bamboo shoots, cut into strips
a few Chinese leaves, cut into strips
60 ml/4 tbsp chicken stock
15 ml/1 tbsp tomato purée (paste)
15 ml/1 tbsp sugar
15 ml/1 tbsp lemon juice

Place the chicken in a bowl. Mix together the lemon juice, soy sauce, wine or sherry and 15 ml/1 tbsp cornflour, pour over the chicken and leave to marinate for 1 hour, turning occasionally.

Heat the oil, salt and garlic until the garlic is lightly browned then add the chicken and marinade and stir-fry for about 5 minutes until the chicken is lightly browned. Add the water chestnuts, bamboo shoots and Chinese leaves and stir-fry for a further 3 minutes or until the chicken is just cooked. Add the remaining ingredients and stir-fry for about 3 minutes until the sauce clears and thickens.

Chicken Livers with Bamboo Shoots

Serves 4

225 g/8 oz chicken livers, thickly sliced
45 ml/3 tbsp rice wine or dry sherry
45 ml/3 tbsp groundnut (peanut) oil
15 ml/1 tbsp soy sauce
100 g/4 oz bamboo shoots, sliced
100 g/4 oz water chestnuts, sliced
60 ml/4 tbsp chicken stock
salt and freshly ground pepper

Mix the chicken livers with the wine or sherry and leave to stand for 30 minutes. Heat the oil and fry the chicken livers until lightly browned. Add the marinade, soy sauce, bamboo shoots, water chestnuts and stock. Bring to the boil and season with salt and pepper. Cover and simmer for about 10 minutes until tender.

Deep-Fried Chicken Livers

Serves 4

450 g/1 lb chicken livers, halved

50 g/2 oz/½ cup cornflour (cornstarch)

oil for deep-frying

Pat the chicken livers dry then dust with cornflour, shaking off any excess. Heat the oil and deep-fry the chicken livers for a few minutes until golden brown and cooked through. Drain on kitchen paper before serving.

Chicken Livers with Mangetout

Serves 4

225 g/8 oz chicken livers, thickly sliced

10 ml/2 tsp cornflour (cornstarch)

10 ml/2 tsp rice wine or dry sherry

15 ml/1 tbsp soy sauce

45 ml/3 tbsp groundnut (peanut) oil

2.5 ml/½ tsp salt

2 slices ginger root, minced

100 g/4 oz mangetout (snow peas)

10 ml/2 tsp cornflour (cornstarch)

60 ml/4 tbsp water

Place the chicken livers in a bowl. Add the cornflour, wine or sherry and soy sauce and toss well to coat. Heat half the oil and fry the salt and ginger until lightly browned. Add the mangetout and stir-fry until well coated with oil then remove from the pan. Heat the remaining oil and fry the chicken livers for 5 minutes until cooked through. Mix the cornflour and water to a paste, stir it into the pan and simmer, stirring, until the sauce clears and thickens. Return the mangetout to the pan and simmer until heated through.

Chicken Livers with Noodle Pancake

Serves 4

30 ml/2 tbsp groundnut (peanut) oil
1 onion, sliced
450 g/1 lb chicken livers, halved
2 stalks celery, sliced
120 ml/4 fl oz/½ cup chicken stock
15 ml/1 tbsp cornflour (cornstarch)
15 ml/1 tbsp soy sauce
30 ml/2 tbsp water
noodle pancake

Heat the oil and fry the onion until softened. Add the chicken livers and stir-fry until coloured. Add the celery and stir-fry for 1 minute. Add the stock, bring to the boil, cover and simmer for 5 minutes. Mix the cornflour, soy sauce and water to a paste, stir it into the pan and simmer, stirring, until the sauce clears and thickens. Pour the mixture over the noodle pancake and serve.

Chicken Livers with Oyster Sauce

Serves 4

45 ml/3 tbsp groundnut (peanut) oil

1 onion, chopped

225 g/8 oz chicken livers, halved

100 g/4 oz mushrooms, sliced

30 ml/2 tbsp oyster sauce

15 ml/1 tbsp soy sauce

15 ml/1 tbsp rice wine or dry sherry

120 ml/4 fl oz/½ cup chicken stock

5 ml/1 tsp sugar

15 ml/1 tbsp cornflour (cornstarch)

45 ml/3 tbsp water

Heat half the oil and fry the onion until softened. Add the chicken livers and fry until just coloured. Add the mushrooms and fry for 2 minutes. Mix the oyster sauce, soy sauce, wine or sherry, stock and sugar, pour it into the pan and bring to the boil, stirring. Mix the cornflour and water to a paste, add it to the pan and simmer, stirring until the sauce clears and thickens and the livers are tender.

Chicken Livers with Pineapple

Serves 4

225 g/8 oz chicken livers, halved
45 ml/3 tbsp groundnut (peanut) oil
30 ml/2 tbsp soy sauce
15 ml/1 tbsp cornflour (cornstarch)
15 ml/1 tbsp sugar
15 ml/1 tbsp wine vinegar
salt and freshly ground pepper
100 g/4 oz pineapple chunks
60 ml/4 tbsp chicken stock

Blanch the chicken livers in boiling water for 30 seconds then drain. Heat the oil and stir-fry the chicken livers for 30 seconds. Mix together the soy sauce, cornflour, sugar, wine vinegar, salt and pepper, pour into the pan and stir well to coat the chicken livers. Add the pineapple chunks and stock and stir-fry for about 3 minutes until the livers are cooked.

Sweet and Sour Chicken Livers

Serves 4

30 ml/2 tbsp groundnut (peanut) oil
450 g/1 lb chicken livers, quartered
2 green peppers, cut into chunks
4 slices canned pineapple, cut into chunks
60 ml/4 tbsp chicken stock
30 ml/2 tbsp cornflour (cornstarch)
10 ml/2 tsp soy sauce
100 g/4 oz/½ cup sugar
120 ml/4 fl oz/½ cup wine vinegar
120 ml/4 fl oz/½ cup water

Heat the oil and fry the livers until lightly browned then transfer them to a warmed serving dish. Add the peppers to the pan and fry for 3 minutes. Add the pineapple and stock, bring to the boil, cover and simmer for 15 minutes. Blend the remaining ingredients to a paste, stir into the pan and simmer, stirring, until the sauce thickens. Pour over the chicken livers and serve.

Chicken with Lychees

Serves 4

3 chicken breasts

60 ml/4 tbsp cornflour (cornstarch)

45 ml/3 tbsp groundnut (peanut) oil

5 spring onions (scallions), sliced

1 red pepper, cut into chunks

120 ml/4 fl oz/½ cup tomato sauce

120 ml/4 fl oz/½ cup chicken stock

5 ml/1 tsp sugar

275 g/10 oz peeled lychees

Cut the chicken breasts in half and remove and discard the bones and skin. Cut each breast into 6. Reserve 5 ml/1 tsp of cornflour and toss the chicken in the remainder until it is well coated. Heat the oil and stir-fry the chicken for about 8 minutes until golden brown. Add the spring onions and pepper and stir-fry for 1 minute. Mix together the tomato sauce, half the stock and the sugar and stir it into the wok with the lychees. Bring to the boil, cover and simmer for about 10 minutes until the chicken is cooked through. Mix the reserved cornflour and stock then stir it into the pan. Simmer, stirring, until the sauce clears and thickens.

Chicken with Lychee Sauce

Serves 4

225 g/8 oz chicken

1 spring onion (scallion)

4 water chestnuts

30 ml/2 tbsp cornflour (cornstarch)

45 ml/3 tbsp soy sauce

30 ml/2 tbsp rice wine or dry sherry

2 egg whites

oil for deep-frying

400 g/14 oz canned lychees in syrup

5 tbsp chicken stock

Mince (grind) the chicken with the spring onion and water chestnuts. Mix in half the cornflour, 30 ml/2 tbsp of soy sauce, the wine or sherry and the egg whites. Shape the mixture into walnut-sized balls. Heat the oil and deep-fry the chicken until golden brown. Drain on kitchen paper.

Meanwhile, heat the lychee syrup gently with the stock and reserved soy sauce. Mix the remaining cornflour with a little water, stir it into the pan and simmer, stirring, until the sauce clears and thickens. Stir in the lychees and simmer gently to heat through. Arrange the chicken on a warmed serving plate, pour over the lychees and sauce and serve at once.

Chicken with Mangetout

Serves 4

225 g/8 oz chicken, thinly sliced
5 ml/1 tsp cornflour (cornstarch)
5 ml/1 tsp rice wine or dry sherry
5 ml/1 tsp sesame oil
1 egg white, lightly beaten
45 ml/3 tbsp groundnut (peanut) oil
1 clove garlic, crushed
1 slice ginger root, minced
100 g/4 oz mangetout (snow peas)
120 ml/4 fl oz/½ cup chicken stock
salt and freshly ground pepper

Mix the chicken with the cornflour, wine or sherry, sesame oil and egg white. Heat half the oil and fry the garlic and ginger until lightly browned. Add the chicken and fry until golden then remove from the pan. Heat the remaining oil and fry the mangetout for 2 minutes. Add the stock, bring to the boil, cover and simmer for 2 minutes. Return the chicken to the pan and season with salt and pepper. Simmer gently until heated through.

Chicken with Mangoes

Serves 4

100 g/4 oz/1 cup plain (all-purpose) flour

250 ml/8 fl oz/1 cup water

2.5 ml/½ tsp salt

pinch of baking powder

3 chicken breasts

oil for deep-frying

1 slice ginger root, minced

150 ml/¼ pt/generous ½ cup chicken stock

45 ml/3 tbsp wine vinegar

45 ml/3 tbsp rice wine or dry sherry

20 ml/4 tsp soy sauce

10 ml/2 tsp sugar

10 ml/2 tsp cornflour (cornstarch)

5 ml/1 tsp sesame oil

5 spring onions (scallions), sliced

400 g/11 oz canned mangoes, drained and cut into strips

Whisk together the flour, water, salt and baking powder. Leave to stand for 15 minutes. Remove and discard the skin and bones from the chicken. Cut the chicken into thin strips. Mix these into the flour mixture. Heat the oil and fry the chicken for about 5 minutes until golden brown. Remove from the pan and drain on kitchen paper. Remove all but 15 ml/1 tbsp of oil from the wok and stir-fry the ginger until lightly browned. Mix the stock with the wine vinegar, wine or sherry, soy sauce, sugar, cornflour and sesame oil. Add to the pan and bring to the boil, stirring. Add the spring onions and simmer for 3 minutes. Add the chicken and mangoes and simmer, stirring, for 2 minutes.

Chicken-Stuffed Melon

Serves 4

350 g/12 oz chicken meat
6 water chestnuts
2 shelled scallops
4 slices ginger root
5 ml/1 tsp salt
15 ml/1 tbsp soy sauce
600 ml/1 pt/2½ cups chicken stock
8 small or 4 medium cantaloupe melons

Finely chop the chicken, chestnuts, scallops and ginger and mix with the salt, soy sauce and stock. Cut the tops off the melons and scoop out the seeds. Serrate the top edges. Fill the melons with the chicken mixture and stand on a rack in a steamer. Steam over boiling water for 40 minutes until the chicken is cooked.

Chicken and Mushroom Stir-Fry

Serves 4

45 ml/3 tbsp groundnut (peanut) oil
1 clove garlic, crushed
1 spring onion (scallion), chopped
1 slice ginger root, minced
225 g/8 oz chicken breast, cut into slivers
225 g/8 oz button mushrooms
45 ml/3 tbsp soy sauce
15 ml/1 tbsp rice wine or dry sherry
5 ml/1 tsp cornflour (cornstarch)

Heat the oil and fry the garlic, spring onion and ginger until lightly browned. Add the chicken and stir-fry for 5 minutes. Add the mushrooms and stir-fry for 3 minutes. Add the soy sauce, wine or sherry and cornflour and stir-fry for about 5 minutes until the chicken is cooked through.

Chicken with Mushrooms and Peanuts

Serves 4

30 ml/2 tbsp groundnut (peanut) oil

2 cloves garlic, crushed

1 slice ginger root, minced

450 g/1 lb boned chicken, cubed

225 g/8 oz button mushrooms

100 g/4 oz bamboo shoots, cut into strips

1 green pepper, cubed

1 red pepper, cubed

250 ml/8 fl oz/1 cup chicken stock

30 ml/2 tbsp rice wine or dry sherry

15 ml/1 tbsp soy sauce

15 ml/1 tbsp tabasco sauce

30 ml/2 tbsp cornflour (cornstarch)

30 ml/2 tbsp water

Heat the oil, garlic and ginger until the garlic is lightly golden. Add the chicken and stir-fry until it is lightly browned. Add the mushrooms, bamboo shoots and peppers and stir-fry for 3 minutes. Add the stock, wine or sherry, soy sauce and tabasco sauce and bring to the boil, stirring. Cover and simmer for about 10 minutes until the chicken is thoroughly cooked. Mix together the cornflour and water and stir them into the sauce. Simmer, stirring, until the sauce clears and thickens, adding a little more stock or water if the sauce is too thick.

Stir-Fried Chicken with Mushrooms

Serves 4

6 dried Chinese mushrooms
1 chicken breast, thinly sliced
1 slice ginger root, minced
2 spring onions (scallions), minced
15 ml/1 tbsp cornflour (cornstarch)
15 ml/1 tbsp rice wine or dry sherry
30 ml/2 tbsp water
2.5 ml/½ tsp salt
45 ml/3 tbsp groundnut (peanut) oil
225 g/8 oz mushrooms, sliced
100 g/4 oz bean sprouts
15 ml/1 tbsp soy sauce
5 ml/1 tsp sugar
120 ml/4 fl oz/½ cup chicken stock

Soak the mushrooms in warm water for 30 minutes then drain. Discard the stalks and slice the caps. Place the chicken in a bowl. Mix the ginger, spring onions, cornflour, wine or sherry, water and salt, stir into the chicken and leave to stand for 1 hour. Heat half the oil and stir-fry the chicken until lightly browned then remove it from the pan. Heat the remaining oil and stir-fry the dried and fresh mushrooms and the bean sprouts for 3 minutes. Add the soy sauce, sugar and stock, bring to the boil, cover and simmer for 4 minutes until the vegetables are just tender. Return the chicken to the pan, stir well and reheat gently before serving.

Steamed Chicken with Mushrooms

Serves 4

4 chicken pieces
30 ml/2 tbsp cornflour (cornstarch)
30 ml/2 tbsp soy sauce
3 spring onions (scallions), chopped
2 slices root ginger, chopped
2.5 ml/½ tsp salt
100 g/4 oz mushrooms, sliced

Chop the chicken pieces into 5 cm/2 in chunks and place them in an ovenproof bowl. Mix the cornflour and soy sauce to a paste, stir in the spring onions, ginger and salt and mix well with the chicken. Gently stir in the mushrooms. Place the bowl on a rack in a steamer, cover and steam over boiling water for about 35 minutes until the chicken is tender.

Chicken with Onions

Serves 4

60 ml/4 tbsp groundnut (peanut) oil
2 onions, chopped
450 g/1 lb chicken, sliced
30 ml/2 tbsp rice wine or dry sherry
250 ml/8 fl oz/1 cup chicken stock
45 ml/3 tbsp soy sauce
30 ml/2 tbsp cornflour (cornstarch)
45 ml/3 tbsp water

Heat the oil and fry the onions until lightly browned. Add the chicken and fry until lightly browned. Add the wine or sherry, stock and soy sauce, bring to the boil, cover and simmer for 25 minutes until the chicken is tender. Blend the cornflour and water to a paste, stir it into the pan and simmer, stirring, until the sauce clears and thickens.

Orange and Lemon Chicken

Serves 4

350 g/1 lb chicken meat, cut into strips
30 ml/2 tbsp groundnut (peanut) oil
2 cloves garlic, crushed
2 slices ginger root, minced
grated rind of ½ orange
grated rind of ½ lemon
45 ml/3 tbsp orange juice
45 ml/3 tbsp lemon juice
15 ml/1 tbsp soy sauce
3 spring onions (scallions), chopped
15 ml/1 tbsp cornflour (cornstarch)
45 ml/1 tbsp water

Blanch the chicken in boiling water for 30 seconds then drain. Heat the oil and stir-fry the garlic and ginger for 30 seconds. Add the orange and lemon rind and juice, soy sauce and spring onions and stir-fry for 2 minutes. Add the chicken and simmer for a few minutes until the chicken is tender. Blend the cornflour and water to a paste, stir into the pan and simmer, stirring, until the sauce thickens.

Chicken with Oyster Sauce

Serves 4

30 ml/2 tbsp groundnut (peanut) oil
1 clove garlic, crushed
1 slice ginger, finely chopped
450 g/1 lb chicken, sliced
250 ml/8 fl oz/1 cup chicken stock
30 ml/2 tbsp oyster sauce
15 ml/1 tbsp rice wine or sherry
5 ml/1 tsp sugar

Heat the oil with the garlic and ginger and fry until lightly browned. Add the chicken and stir-fry for about 3 minutes until lightly browned. Add the stock, oyster sauce, wine or sherry and sugar, bring to the boil, stirring, then cover and simmer for about 15 minutes, stirring occasionally, until the chicken is cooked through. Remove the lid and continue to cook, stirring, for about 4 minutes until the sauce has reduced and thickened.

Chicken Parcels

Serves 4

225 g/8 oz chicken
30 ml/2 tbsp rice wine or dry sherry
30 ml/2 tbsp soy sauce
waxed paper or baking parchment
30 ml/2 tbsp groundnut (peanut) oil
oil for deep-frying

Cut the chicken into 5 cm/2 in cubes. Mix the wine or sherry and soy sauce, pour over the chicken and stir well. Cover and leave to stand for 1 hour, stirring occasionally. Cut the paper into 10 cm/4 in squares and brush with oil. Drain the chicken well. Place a piece of paper on the work surface with one corner pointing towards you. Place a piece of chicken on the square just below the centre, fold up the bottom corner and fold up again to encase the chicken. Fold in the sides then fold down the top corner to secure the parcel. Heat the oil and deep-fry the chicken parcels for about 5 minutes until cooked. Serve hot in the parcels for the guests to open themselves.

Chicken with Peanuts

Serves 4

225 g/8 oz chicken, thinly sliced

1 egg white, lightly beaten

10 ml/2 tsp cornflour (cornstarch)

45 ml/3 tbsp groundnut (peanut) oil

1 clove garlic, crushed

1 slice ginger root, minced

2 leeks, chopped

30 ml/2 tbsp soy sauce

15 ml/1 tbsp rice wine or dry sherry

100 g/4 oz roasted peanuts

Mix the chicken with the egg white and cornflour until well coated. Heat half the oil and stir-fry the chicken until golden brown then remove from the pan. Heat the remaining oil and fry and garlic and ginger until softened. Add the leeks and fry until lightly browned. Stir in the soy sauce and wine or sherry and simmer for 3 minutes. Return the chicken to the pan with the peanuts and simmer gently until heated through.

Chicken with Peanut Butter

Serves 4

4 chicken breasts, diced
salt and freshly ground pepper
5 ml/1 tsp five-spice powder
45 ml/3 tbsp groundnut (peanut) oil
1 onion, diced
2 carrots, diced
1 stick celery, diced
300 ml/½ pt/1¼ cups chicken stock
10 ml/2 tsp tomato purée (paste)
100 g/4 oz peanut butter
15 ml/1 tbsp soy sauce
10 ml/2 tsp cornflour (cornstarch)
pinch of brown sugar
15 ml/1 tbsp chopped chives

Season the chicken with salt, pepper and five-spice powder. Heat the oil and stir-fry the chicken until tender. Remove from the pan. Add the vegetables and fry until tender but still crisp. Mix the stock with the remaining ingredients except the chives, stir into the pan and bring to the boil. Return the chicken to the pan and reheat, stirring. Serve sprinkled with sugar.

Chicken with Peas

Serves 4

60 ml/4 tbsp groundnut (peanut) oil
1 onion, chopped
450 g/1 lb chicken, diced
salt and freshly ground pepper
100 g/4 oz peas
2 stalks celery, chopped
100 g/4 oz mushrooms, chopped
250 ml/8 fl oz/1 cup chicken stock
15 ml/1 tbsp cornflour (cornstarch)
15 ml/1 tbsp soy sauce
60 ml/4 tbsp water

Heat the oil and fry the onion until lightly browned. Add the chicken and fry until coloured. Season with salt and pepper and add the peas, celery and mushrooms and stir well. Add the stock, bring to the boil, cover and simmer for 15 minutes. Blend the cornflour, soy sauce and water to a paste, stir it into the pan and simmer, stirring, until the sauce clears and thickens.

Peking Chicken

Serves 4

4 chicken portions
salt and freshly ground pepper
5 ml/1 tsp sugar
1 spring onion (scallion), chopped
1 slice ginger root, minced
15 ml/1 tbsp soy sauce
15 ml/1 tbsp rice wine or dry sherry
15 ml/1 tbsp cornflour (cornstarch)
oil for deep-frying

Place the chicken portions in a shallow bowl and sprinkle with salt and pepper. Mix the sugar, spring onion, ginger, soy sauce and wine or sherry, rub into the chicken, cover and leave to marinate for 3 hours. Drain the chicken and dust it with cornflour. Heat the oil and deep-fry the chicken until golden brown and cooked through. Drain well before serving.

Chicken with Peppers

Serves 4

60 ml/4 tbsp soy sauce

45 ml/3 tbsp rice wine or dry sherry

45 ml/3 tbsp cornflour (cornstarch)

450 g/1 lb chicken, minced (ground)

60 ml/4 tbsp groundnut (peanut) oil

2.5 ml/½ tsp salt

2 cloves garlic, crushed

2 red peppers, cubed

1 green pepper, cubed

5 ml/1 tsp sugar

300 ml/½ pt/1¼ cups chicken stock

Mix together half the soy sauce, half the wine or sherry and half the cornflour. Pour over the chicken, stir well, and leave to marinate for at least 1 hour. Heat half the oil with the salt and garlic until the garlic is lightly browned. Add the chicken and marinade and stir-fry for about 4 minutes until the chicken turns white then remove from the pan. Add the remaining oil to the pan and stir-fry the peppers for 2 minutes. Add the sugar to the pan with the remaining soy sauce, wine or sherry and cornflour and mix well. Add the stock, bring to the boil then simmer, stirring, until the sauce thickens. Return the chicken to the pan, cover and simmer for 4 minutes until the chicken is cooked through.

Stir-Fried Chicken with Peppers

Serves 4

1 chicken breast, thinly sliced
2 slices ginger root, minced
2 spring onions (scallions), minced
15 ml/1 tbsp cornflour (cornstarch)
30 ml/2 tbsp rice wine or dry sherry
30 ml/2 tbsp water
2.5 ml/½ tsp salt
45 ml/3 tbsp groundnut (peanut) oil
100 g/4 oz water chestnuts, sliced
1 red pepper, cut into strips
1 green pepper, cut into strips
1 yellow pepper, cut into strips
30 ml/2 tbsp soy sauce
120 ml/4 fl oz/½ cup chicken stock

Place the chicken in a bowl. Mix the ginger, spring onions, cornflour, wine or sherry, water and salt, stir into the chicken and leave to stand for 1 hour. Heat half the oil and stir-fry the chicken until lightly browned then remove it from the pan. Heat the remaining oil and stir-fry the water chestnuts and peppers for 2 minutes. Add the soy sauce and stock, bring to the boil, cover and simmer for 5 minutes until the vegetables are just tender. Return the chicken to the pan, stir well and reheat gently before serving.

Chicken and Pineapple

Serves 4

30 ml/2 tbsp groundnut (peanut) oil

5 ml/1 tsp salt

2 cloves garlic, crushed

450 g/1 lb boned chicken, thinly sliced

2 onions, sliced

100 g/4 oz water chestnuts, sliced

100 g/4 oz pineapple chunks

30 ml/2 tbsp rice wine or dry sherry

450 ml/¾ pt/2 cups chicken stock

5 ml/1 tsp sugar

freshly ground pepper

30 ml/2 tbsp pineapple juice

30 ml/2 tbsp soy sauce

30 ml/2 tbsp cornflour (cornstarch)

Heat the oil, salt and garlic until the garlic turns light golden. Add the chicken and stir-fry for 2 minutes. Add the onions, water chestnuts and pineapple and stir-fry for 2 minutes. Add the wine or sherry, stock and sugar and season with pepper. Bring to the boil, cover and simmer for 5 minutes. Mix together the pineapple juice, soy sauce and cornflour. Stir into the pan and simmer, stirring until the sauce thickens and clears.

Chicken with Pineapple and Lychees

Serves 4

30 ml/2 tbsp groundnut (peanut) oil
225 g/8 oz chicken, thinly sliced
1 slice ginger root, minced
15 ml/1 tbsp soy sauce
15 ml/1 tbsp rice wine or dry sherry
200 g/7 oz canned pineapple chunks in syrup
200 g/7 oz canned lychees in syrup
15 ml/1 tbsp cornflour (cornstarch)

Heat the oil and fry the chicken until lightly coloured. Add the soy sauce and wine or sherry and stir well. Measure 250 ml/8 fl oz/1 cup of the mixed pineapple and lychee syrup and reserve 30 ml/2 tbsp. Add the rest to the pan, bring to the boil and simmer for a few minutes until the chicken is tender. Add the pineapple chunks and lychees. Mix the cornflour with the reserved syrup, stir into the pan and simmer, stirring, until the sauce clears and thickens.

Chicken with Pork

Serves 4

1 chicken breast, thinly sliced
100 g/4 oz lean pork, thinly sliced
60 ml/4 tbsp soy sauce
15 ml/1 tbsp cornflour (cornstarch)
1 egg white
45 ml/3 tbsp groundnut (peanut) oil
3 slices ginger root, chopped
50 g/2 oz bamboo shoots, sliced
225 g/8 oz mushrooms, sliced
225 g/8 oz Chinese leaves, shredded
120 ml/4 fl oz/½ cup chicken stock
30 ml/2 tbsp water

Mix together the chicken and pork. Mix the soy sauce, 5 ml/1 tsp of cornflour and the egg white and stir into the chicken and pork. Leave to stand for 30 minutes. Heat half the oil and fry the chicken and pork until lightly browned then remove them from the pan. Heat the remaining oil and fry the ginger, bamboo shoots, mushrooms and Chinese leaves until well coated in oil. Add the stock and bring to the boil. Return the chicken mixture to the pan, cover and simmer for about 3 minutes until the meats are tender. Blend the remaining cornflour to a paste with the water, stir into the sauce and simmer, stirring, until the sauce thickens. Serve at once.

Braised Chicken with Potatoes

Serves 4

4 chicken pieces
45 ml/3 tbsp groundnut (peanut) oil
1 onion, sliced
1 clove garlic, crushed
2 slices ginger root, minced
450 ml/¾ pt/2 cups water
45 ml/3 tbsp soy sauce
15 ml/1 tbsp brown sugar
2 potatoes, cubed

Chop the chicken into 5 cm/2 in pieces. Heat the oil and fry the onion, garlic and ginger until lightly browned. Add the chicken and fry until lightly browned. Add the water and soy sauce and bring to the boil. Stir in the sugar, cover and simmer for about 30 minutes. Add the potatoes to the pan, cover and simmer for a further 10 minutes until the chicken is tender and the potatoes are cooked.

Five-Spice Chicken with Potatoes

Serves 4

45 ml/3 tbsp groundnut (peanut) oil
450 g/1 lb chicken, cut into chunks
salt
45 ml/3 tbsp yellow bean paste
45 ml/3 tbsp soy sauce
5 ml/1 tsp sugar
5 ml/1 tsp five-spice powder
1 potato, diced
450 ml/¾ pt/2 cups chicken stock

Heat the oil and stir-fry the chicken until lightly browned. Sprinkle with salt then stir in the bean paste, soy sauce, sugar and five-spice powder and stir-fry for 1 minute. Add the potato and stir in well then add the stock, bring to the boil, cover and simmer for about 30 minutes until tender.

Red-Cooked Chicken

Serves 4

450 g/1 lb chicken, sliced
120 ml/4 fl oz/½ cup soy sauce
15 ml/1 tbsp sugar
2 slices ginger root, finely chopped
90 ml/6 tbsp chicken stock
30 ml/2 tbsp rice wine or dry sherry
4 spring onions (scallions), sliced

Place all the ingredients in a pan and bring to the boil. Cover and simmer for about 15 minutes until the chicken is cooked through. Remove the lid and continue to simmer for about 5 minutes, stirring occasionally, until the sauce has thickened. Serve sprinkled with spring onions.

Chicken Rissoles

Serves 4

225 g/8 oz chicken meat, minced (ground)
3 water chestnuts, minced
1 spring onion (scallion), chopped
1 slice ginger root, minced
2 egg whites
5 ml/2 tsp salt
5 ml/1 tsp freshly ground pepper
120 ml/4 fl oz/½ cup groundnut (peanut) oil
5 ml/1 tsp chopped ham

Mix together the chicken, chestnuts, half the spring onion, the ginger, egg whites, salt and pepper. Shape into small balls and press flat. Heat the oil and fry the rissoles until golden brown, turning once. Serve sprinkled with the remaining spring onion and the ham.

Savoury Chicken

Serves 4

30 ml/2 tbsp groundnut (peanut) oil

4 chicken pieces

3 spring onions (scallions), chopped

2 cloves garlic, crushed

1 slice ginger root, chopped

120 ml/4 fl oz/½ cup soy sauce

30 ml/2 tbsp rice wine or dry sherry

30 ml/2 tbsp brown sugar

5 ml/1 tsp salt

375 ml/13 fl oz/1½ cups water

15 ml/1 tbsp cornflour (cornstarch)

Heat the oil and fry the chicken pieces until golden brown. Add the spring onions, garlic and ginger and fry for 2 minutes. Add the soy sauce, wine or sherry, sugar and salt and stir together well. Add the water and bring to the boil, cover and simmer for 40 minutes. Mix the cornflour with a little water, stir it into the sauce and simmer, stirring, until the sauce clears and thickens.

Chicken in Sesame Oil

Serves 4

90 ml/6 tbsp groundnut (peanut) oil

60 ml/4 tbsp sesame oil

5 slices ginger root

4 chicken pieces

600 ml/1 pt/2½ cups rice wine or dry sherry

5 ml/1 tsp sugar

salt and freshly ground pepper

Heat the oils and fry the ginger and chicken until lightly browned. Add the wine or sherry and season with sugar, salt and pepper. Bring to the boil and simmer gently, uncovered, until the chicken is tender and the sauce has reduced. Serve in bowls.

Sherry Chicken

Serves 4

30 ml/2 tbsp groundnut (peanut) oil

4 chicken pieces

120 ml/4 fl oz/½ cup soy sauce

500 ml/17 fl oz/2¼ cups rice wine or dry sherry

30 ml/2 tbsp sugar

5 ml/1 tsp salt

2 cloves garlic, crushed

1 slice ginger root, chopped

Heat the oil and fry the chicken until browned on all sides. Drain off excess oil and add all the remaining ingredients. Bring to the boil, cover and simmer over a fairly high heat for 25 minutes. Reduce the heat and simmer for a further 15 minutes until the chicken is cooked through and the sauce has reduced.

Chicken with Soy Sauce

Serves 4

350 g/12 oz chicken, diced

2 spring onions (scallions), chopped

3 slices ginger root, minced

15 ml/1 tbsp cornflour (cornstarch)

30 ml/2 tbsp rice wine or dry sherry

30 ml/2 tbsp water

45 ml/3 tbsp groundnut (peanut) oil

60 ml/4 tbsp thick soy sauce

5 ml/1 tsp sugar

Mix together the chicken, spring onions, ginger, cornflour, wine or sherry and water and leave to stand for 30 minutes, stirring occasionally. Heat the oil and stir-fry the chicken for about 3 minutes until lightly browned. Add the soy sauce and sugar and stir-fry for about 1 minute until the chicken is cooked through and tender.

Spicy Baked Chicken

Serves 4

150 ml/¼ pt/generous ½ cup soy sauce

2 cloves garlic, crushed

50 g/2 oz/¼ cup brown sugar

1 onion, finely chopped

30 ml/2 tbsp tomato purée (paste)

1 slice lemon, chopped

1 slice ginger root, minced

45 ml/3 tbsp rice wine or dry sherry

4 large chicken pieces

Mix together all the ingredients except the chicken. Place the chicken in an ovenproof dish, pour over the mixture, cover and marinate overnight, basting occasionally. Bake the chicken in a preheated oven at 180°C/350°F/gas mark 4 for 40 minutes, turning and basting occasionally. Remove the lid, raise the oven temperature to 200°C/400°F/gas mark 6 and continue to cook for a further 15 minutes until the chicken is cooked through.

Chicken with Spinach

Serves 4

100 g/4 oz chicken, minced
15 ml/1 tbsp ham fat, minced
175 ml/6 fl oz/¾ cup chicken stock
3 egg whites, lightly beaten
salt
5 ml/1 tsp water
450 g/1 lb spinach, finely chopped
5 ml/1 tsp cornflour (cornstarch)
45 ml/3 tbsp groundnut (peanut) oil

Mix together the chicken, ham fat, 150 ml/¼ pt/generous ½ cup of chicken stock, the egg whites, 5 ml/1 tsp of salt and the water. Mix the spinach with the remaining stock, a pinch of salt and the cornflour mixed with a little water. Heat half the oil, add the spinach mixture to the pan and stir constantly over a low heat until heated through. Transfer to a warmed serving plate and keep warm. Heat the remaining oil and fry spoonfuls of the chicken mixture until set and white. Arrange on top of the spinach and serve at once.

Chicken Spring Rolls

Serves 4

15 ml/1 tbsp groundnut (peanut) oil
pinch of salt
1 clove garlic, crushed
225 g/8 oz chicken, cut into strips
100 g/4 oz mushrooms, sliced
175 g/6 oz cabbage, shredded
100 g/4 oz bamboo shoots, shredded
50 g/2 oz water chestnuts, shredded
100 g/4 oz bean sprouts
5 ml/1 tsp sugar
5 ml/1 tsp rice wine or dry sherry
5 ml/1 tsp soy sauce
8 spring roll skins
oil for deep-frying

Heat the oil, salt and garlic and fry gently until the garlic begins to turn golden. Add the chicken and mushrooms and stir-fry for a few minutes until the chicken turns white. Add the cabbage, bamboo shoots, water chestnuts and bean sprouts and stir-fry for 3 minutes. Add the sugar, wine or sherry and soy sauce, stir well, cover and stir-fry for a final 2 minutes. Turn into a colander and leave to drain.

Place a few spoonfuls of the filling mixture in the centre of each spring roll skin, fold up the bottom, fold in the sides, then roll upwards, enclosing the filling. Seal the edge with a little flour and water mixture then leave to dry for 30 minutes. Heat the oil and deep-fry the spring rolls for about 10 minutes until crisp and golden brown. Drain well before serving.

Simple Chicken Stir-Fry

Serves 4

1 chicken breast, thinly sliced
2 slices ginger root, minced
2 spring onions (scallions), minced
15 ml/1 tbsp cornflour (cornstarch)
15 ml/1 tbsp rice wine or dry sherry
30 ml/2 tbsp water
2.5 ml/½ tsp salt
45 ml/3 tbsp groundnut (peanut) oil
100 g/4 oz bamboo shoots, sliced
100 g/4 oz mushrooms, sliced
100 g/4 oz bean sprouts
15 ml/1 tbsp soy sauce
5 ml/1 tsp sugar
120 ml/4 fl oz/½ cup chicken stock

Place the chicken in a bowl. Mix the ginger, spring onions, cornflour, wine or sherry, water and salt, stir into the chicken and leave to stand for 1 hour. Heat half the oil and stir-fry the chicken until lightly browned then remove it from the pan. Heat the remaining oil and stir-fry the bamboo shoots, mushrooms and bean sprouts for 4 minutes. Add the soy sauce, sugar and stock, bring to the boil, cover and simmer for 5 minutes until the vegetables are just tender. Return the chicken to the pan, stir well and reheat gently before serving.

Chicken in Tomato Sauce

Serves 4

30 ml/2 tbsp groundnut (peanut) oil
5 ml/1 tsp salt
2 cloves garlic, crushed
450 g/1 lb chicken, cubed
300 ml/½ pt/1¼ cups chicken stock
120 ml/4 fl oz/½ cup tomato ketchup (catsup)
15 ml/1 tbsp cornflour (cornstarch)
4 spring onions (scallions), sliced

Heat the oil with the salt and garlic until the garlic is lightly golden. Add the chicken and stir-fry until lightly browned. Add most of the stock, bring to the boil, cover and simmer for about 15 minutes until the chicken is tender. Stir the remaining stock with the ketchup and cornflour and stir it into the pan. Simmer, stirring, until the sauce thickens and clears. If the sauce is too thin, leave it simmering for a while until it has reduced. Add the spring onions and simmer for 2 minutes before serving.

Chicken with Tomatoes

Serves 4

225 g/8 oz chicken, diced

15 ml/1 tbsp cornflour (cornstarch)

15 ml/1 tbsp soy sauce

15 ml/1 tbsp rice wine or dry sherry

45 ml/3 tbsp groundnut (peanut) oil

1 onion, diced

60 ml/4 tbsp chicken stock

5 ml/1 tsp salt

5 ml/1 tsp sugar

2 tomatoes, skinned and diced

Mix the chicken with the cornflour, soy sauce and wine or sherry and leave to stand for 30 minutes. Heat the oil and fry the chicken until lightly coloured. Add the onion and stir-fry until softened. Add the stock, salt and sugar, bring to the boil and stir gently over a low heat until the chicken is cooked. Add the tomatoes and stir until heated through.

Poached Chicken with Tomatoes

Serves 4

4 chicken portions

4 tomatoes, skinned and quartered

15 ml/1 tbsp rice wine or dry sherry

15 ml/1 tbsp groundnut (peanut) oil

salt

Place the chicken in a pan and just cover with cold water. Bring to the boil, cover and simmer for 20 minutes. Add the tomatoes, wine or sherry, oil and salt, cover and simmer for a further 10 minutes until the chicken is cooked. Arrange the chicken on a warmed serving plate and chop into serving pieces. Reheat the sauce and pour over the chicken to serve.

Chicken and Tomatoes with Black Bean Sauce

Serves 4

45 ml/3 tbsp groundnut (peanut) oil

1 clove garlic, crushed

45 ml/3 tbsp black bean sauce

225 g/8 oz chicken, diced

15 ml/1 tbsp rice wine or dry sherry

5 ml/1 tsp sugar

15 ml/1 tbsp soy sauce

90 ml/6 tbsp chicken stock

3 tomatoes, skinned and quartered

10 ml/2 tsp cornflour (cornstarch)

45 ml/3 tbsp water

Heat the oil and fry the garlic for 30 seconds. Add the black bean sauce and fry for 30 seconds then add the chicken and stir until well coated in oil. Add the wine or sherry, sugar, soy sauce and stock, bring to the boil, cover and simmer for about 5 minutes until the chicken is cooked. Mix the cornflour and water to a paste, stir it into the pan and simmer, stirring, until the sauce clears and thickens.

Quick-Cooked Chicken with Vegetables

Serves 4

1 egg white

50 g/2 oz cornflour (cornstarch)

225 g/8 oz chicken breasts, cut into strips

75 ml/5 tbsp groundnut (peanut) oil

200 g/7 oz bamboo shoots, cut into strips

50 g/2 oz bean sprouts

1 green pepper, cut into strips

3 spring onions (scallions), sliced

1 slice ginger root, minced

1 clove garlic, minced

15 ml/1 tbsp rice wine or dry sherry

Beat the egg white and cornflour then dip the chicken strips in the mixture. Heat the oil to moderately hot and fry the chicken for a few minutes until just cooked. Remove from the pan and drain well. Add the bamboo shoots, bean sprouts, pepper, onions, ginger and garlic to the pan and stir-fry for 3 minutes. Add the wine or sherry and return the chicken to the pan. Stir together well and heat through before serving.

Walnut Chicken

Serves 4

45 ml/3 tbsp groundnut (peanut) oil

2 spring onions (scallions), chopped

1 slice ginger root, minced

450 g/1 lb chicken breast, very thinly sliced

50 g/2 oz ham, shredded

30 ml/2 tbsp soy sauce

30 ml/2 tbsp rice wine or dry sherry

5 ml/1 tsp sugar

5 ml/1 tsp salt

100 g/4 oz/1 cup walnuts, chopped

Heat the oil and stir-fry the onions and ginger for 1 minute. Add the chicken and ham and stir-fry for 5 minutes until almost cooked. Add the soy sauce, wine or sherry, sugar and salt and stir-fry for 3 minutes. Add the walnuts and stir-fry for 1 minute until the ingredients are thoroughly blended.

Chicken with Walnuts

Serves 4

100 g/4 oz/1 cup shelled walnuts, halved

oil for deep-frying

45 ml/3 tbsp groundnut (peanut) oil

2 slices ginger root, minced

225 g/8 oz chicken, diced

100 g/4 oz bamboo shoots, sliced

75 ml/5 tbsp chicken stock

Prepare the walnuts, heat the oil and deep-fry the walnuts until golden brown then drain well. Heat the groundnut oil and fry the ginger for 30 seconds. Add the chicken and stir-fry until lightly browned. Add the remaining ingredients, bring to the boil and simmer, stirring, until the chicken is cooked.

Chicken with Water Chestnuts

Serves 4

45 ml/3 tbsp groundnut (peanut) oil

2 cloves garlic, crushed

2 spring onions (scallions), chopped

1 slice ginger root, chopped

225 g/8 oz chicken breast, cut into slivers

100 g/4 oz water chestnuts, cut into slivers

45 ml/3 tbsp soy sauce

15 ml/1 tbsp rice wine or dry sherry

5 ml/1 tsp cornflour (cornstarch)

Heat the oil and fry the garlic, spring onions and ginger until lightly browned. Add the chicken and stir-fry for 5 minutes. Add the water chestnuts and stir-fry for 3 minutes. Add the soy sauce, wine or sherry and cornflour and stir-fry for about 5 minutes until the chicken is cooked through.

Savoury Chicken with Water Chestnuts

Serves 4

30 ml/2 tbsp groundnut (peanut) oil

4 chicken pieces

3 spring onions (scallions), chopped

2 cloves garlic, crushed

1 slice ginger root, chopped

250 ml/8 fl oz/1 cup soy sauce

30 ml/2 tbsp rice wine or dry sherry

30 ml/2 tbsp brown sugar

5 ml/1 tsp salt

375 ml/13 fl oz/1¼ cups water

225 g/8 oz water chestnuts, sliced

15 ml/1 tbsp cornflour (cornstarch)

Heat the oil and fry the chicken pieces until golden brown. Add the spring onions, garlic and ginger and fry for 2 minutes. Add the soy sauce, wine or sherry, sugar and salt and stir together well. Add the water and bring to the boil, cover and simmer for 20 minutes. Add the water chestnuts, cover and cook for a further 20 minutes. Mix the cornflour with a little water, stir it into the sauce and simmer, stirring, until the sauce clears and thickens.

Chicken Wontons

Serves 4

4 dried Chinese mushrooms

450 g/1 lb chicken breast, shredded

225 g/8 oz mixed vegetables, chopped

1 spring onion (scallion), chopped

15 ml/1 tbsp soy sauce

2.5 ml/½ tsp salt

40 wonton skins

1 egg, beaten

Soak the mushrooms in warm water for 30 minutes then drain. Discard the stalks and chop the caps. Mix with the chicken, vegetables, soy sauce and salt.

To fold the wontons, hold the skin in the palm of your left hand and spoon a little filling into the centre. Moisten the edges with egg and fold the skin into a triangle, sealing the edges. Moisten the corners with egg and twist them together.

Bring a saucepan of water to the boil. Drop in the wontons and simmer for about 10 minutes until they float to the top.

Crispy Chicken Wings

Serves 4

900 g/2 lb chicken wings
60 ml/4 tbsp rice wine or dry sherry
60 ml/4 tbsp soy sauce
50 g/2 oz/½ cup cornflour (cornstarch)
groundnut (peanut) oil for deep-frying

Place the chicken wings in a bowl. Mix together the remaining ingredients and pour over the chicken wings, stirring well so that they are coated in the sauce. Cover and leave to stand for 30 minutes. Heat the oil and deep-fry the chicken a few at a time until cooked through and dark brown. Drain well on kitchen paper and keep warm while you fry the remaining chicken.

Five-Spice Chicken Wings

Serves 4

30 ml/2 tbsp groundnut (peanut) oil

2 cloves garlic, crushed

450 g/1 lb chicken wings

250 ml/8 fl oz/1 cup chicken stock

30 ml/2 tbsp soy sauce

5 ml/1 tsp sugar

5 ml/1 tsp five-spice powder

Heat the oil and garlic until the garlic is lightly browned. Add the chicken and fry until lightly browned. Add the remaining ingredients, stirring well, and bring to the boil. Cover and simmer for about 15 minutes until the chicken is cooked through. Remove the lid and continue to simmer, stirring occasionally, until almost all the liquid has evaporated. Serve hot or cold.

Marinated Chicken Wings

Serves 4

45 ml/3 tbsp soy sauce

45 ml/3 tbsp rice wine or dry sherry

30 ml/2 tbsp brown sugar

5 ml/1 tsp grated ginger root

2 cloves garlic, crushed

6 spring onions (scallions), sliced

450 g/1 lb chicken wings

30 ml/2 tbsp groundnut (peanut) oil

225 g/8 oz bamboo shoots, sliced

20 ml/4 tsp cornflour (cornstarch)

175 ml/6 fl oz/¾ cup chicken stock

Mix together the soy sauce, wine or sherry, sugar, ginger, garlic and spring onions. Add the chicken wings and stir to coat completely. Cover and leave to stand for 1 hour, stirring occasionally. Heat the oil and stir-fry the bamboo shoots for 2 minutes. Remove them from the pan. Drain the chicken and onions, reserving the marinade. Reheat the oil and stir-fry the chicken until browned on all sides. Cover and cook for a further 20 minutes until the chicken is tender. Blend the cornflour with the stock and the reserved marinade. Pour over the chicken and bring to the boil, stirring, until the sauce thickens. Stir in the bamboo shoots and simmer, stirring, for a further 2 minutes.

Royal Chicken Wings

Serves 4

12 chicken wings
250 ml/8 fl oz/1 cup groundnut (peanut) oil
15 ml/1 tbsp granulated sugar
2 spring onions (scallions), cut into chunks
5 slices root ginger
5 ml/1 tsp salt
45 ml/3 tbsp soy sauce
250 ml/8 fl oz/1 cup rice wine or dry sherry
250 ml/8 fl oz/1 cup chicken stock
10 slices bamboo shoots
15 ml/1 tbsp cornflour (cornstarch)
15 ml/1 tbsp water
2.5 ml/½ tsp sesame oil

Blanch the chicken wings in boiling water for 5 minutes then drain well. Heat the oil, add the sugar and stir until melted and golden brown. Add the chicken, spring onions, ginger, salt, soy sauce, wine and stock, bring to the boil and simmer gently for 20 minutes. Add the bamboo shoots and simmer for 2 minutes or until the liquid has almost all evaporated. Blend the cornflour with the water, stir it into the pan and stir until thick. Transfer the chicken wings to a warmed serving plate and serve sprinkled with sesame oil.

Spiced Chicken Wings

Serves 4

30 ml/2 tbsp groundnut (peanut) oil
5 ml/1 tsp salt
2 cloves garlic, crushed
900 g/2 lb chicken wings
30 ml/2 tbsp rice wine or dry sherry
30 ml/2 tbsp soy sauce
30 ml/2 tbsp tomato purée (paste)
15 ml/1 tbsp Worcestershire sauce

Heat the oil, salt and garlic and fry until the garlic turns light golden. Add the chicken wings and fry, stirring frequently, for about 10 minutes until golden brown and almost cooked through. Add the remaining ingredients and stir-fry for about 5 minutes until the chicken is crispy and thoroughly cooked.

Barbecued Chicken Drumsticks

Serves 4

16 chicken drumsticks

30 ml/2 tbsp rice wine or dry sherry

30 ml/2 tbsp wine vinegar

30 ml/2 tbsp olive oil

salt and freshly ground pepper

120 ml/4 fl oz/½ cup orange juice

30 ml/2 tbsp soy sauce

30 ml/2 tbsp honey

15 ml/1 tbsp lemon juice

2 slices ginger root, minced

120 ml/4 fl oz/½ cup chilli sauce

Mix together all the ingredients except the chilli sauce, cover and leave to marinate in the refrigerator overnight. Remove the chicken from the marinade and barbecue or grill (broil) for about 25 minutes, turning and basting with the chilli sauce as you cook.

Hoisin Chicken Drumsticks

Serves 4

8 chicken drumsticks
600 ml/1 pt/2½ cups chicken stock
salt and freshly ground pepper
250 ml/8 fl oz/1 cup hoisin sauce
30 ml/2 tbsp plain (all-purpose) flour
2 eggs, beaten
100 g/4 oz/1 cup breadcrumbs
oil for deep-frying

Place the drumsticks and stock in a pan, bring to the boil, cover and simmer for 20 minutes until cooked. Remove the chicken from the pan and pat dry on kitchen paper. Place the chicken in a bowl and season with salt and pepper. Pour over the hoisin sauce and leave to marinate for 1 hour. Drain. Toss the chicken in the flour then coat in the eggs and breadcrumbs, then in egg and breadcrumbs again. Heat the oil and fry the chicken for about 5 minutes until golden brown. Drain on kitchen paper and serve hot or cold.

Braised Chicken

Serves 4–6

75 ml/5 tbsp groundnut (peanut) oil
1 chicken
3 spring onions (scallions), sliced
3 slices ginger root
120 ml/4 fl oz/½ cup soy sauce
30 ml/2 tbsp rice wine or dry sherry
5 ml/1 tsp sugar

Heat the oil and fry the chicken until browned. Add the spring onions, ginger, soy sauce and wine or sherry, and bring to the boil. Cover and simmer for 30 minutes, turning occasionally. Add the sugar, cover and simmer for a further 30 minutes until the chicken is cooked.

Crispy-Fried Chicken

Serves 4

1 chicken

salt

30 ml/2 tbsp rice wine or dry sherry

3 spring onions (scallions), diced

1 slice ginger root

30 ml/2 tbsp soy sauce

30 ml/2 tbsp sugar

5 ml/1 tsp whole cloves

5 ml/1 tsp salt

5 ml/1 tsp peppercorns

150 ml/¼ pt/generous ½ cup chicken stock

oil for deep-frying

1 lettuce, shredded

4 tomatoes, sliced

½ cucumber, sliced

Rub the chicken with salt and leave to stand for 3 hours. Rinse and place in a bowl. Add the wine or sherry, ginger, soy sauce, sugar, cloves, salt, peppercorns and stock and baste well. Stand the bowl in a steamer, cover and steam for about 2¼ hours until the chicken is thoroughly cooked. Drain. Heat the oil until smoking, then add the chicken and deep-fry until browned. Fry for a further 5 minutes then remove from the oil and drain. Cut into pieces and arrange on a warmed serving plate. Garnish with the lettuce, tomatoes and cucumber and serve with a pepper and salt dip.

Deep-Fried Whole Chicken

Serves 5

1 chicken

10 ml/2 tsp salt

15 ml/1 tbsp rice wine or dry sherry

2 spring onions (scallions), halved

3 slices ginger root, cut into strips

oil for deep-frying

Pat the chicken dry and rub the skin with salt and wine or sherry. Place the spring onions and ginger inside the cavity. Hang the chicken to dry in a cool place for about 3 hours. Heat the oil and place the chicken in a frying basket. Lower gently into the oil and baste continuously inside and out until the chicken is lightly coloured. Remove from the oil and leave to cool slightly while you reheat the oil. Fry again until golden brown. Drain well then chop into pieces.

Five-Spice Chicken

Serves 4–6

1 chicken
120 ml/4 fl oz/½ cup soy sauce
2.5 cm/1 in piece ginger root, minced
1 clove garlic, crushed
15 ml/1 tbsp five-spice powder
30 ml/2 tbsp rice wine or dry sherry
30 ml/2 tbsp honey
2.5 ml/½ tsp sesame oil
oil for deep-frying
30 ml/2 tbsp salt
5 ml/1 tsp freshly ground pepper

Place the chicken in a large saucepan and fill with water to come half way up the thigh. Reserve 15 ml/1 tbsp of the soy sauce and add the remainder to the pan with the ginger, garlic and half the five-spice powder. Bring to the boil, cover and simmer for 5 minutes. Turn off the heat and leave the chicken to stand in the water until the water is lukewarm. Drain.

Cut the chicken in half lengthways and place cut side down in a roasting tin. Mix together the remaining soy sauce and five-spice powder with the wine or sherry, honey and sesame oil. Rub the mixture over the chicken and leave to stand for 2 hours, brushing occasionally with the mixture. Heat the oil and deep-fry the chicken halves for about 15 minutes until golden brown and cooked through. Drain on kitchen paper and cut into serving sized pieces.

Meanwhile, mix the salt and pepper and heat in a dry pan for about 2 minutes. Serve as a dip with the chicken.

Ginger and Spring Onion Chicken

Serves 4

1 chicken

2 slices ginger root, cut into strips

salt and freshly ground pepper

90 ml/4 tbsp groundnut (peanut) oil

8 spring onions (scallions), finely chopped

10 ml/2 tsp white wine vinegar

5 ml/1 tsp soy sauce

Place the chicken in a large saucepan, add half the ginger and pour in enough water almost to cover the chicken. Season with salt and pepper. Bring to the boil, cover and simmer for about 1¼ hours until tender. Leave the chicken to stand in the stock until cool. Drain the chicken and refrigerate until cold. Cut into portions.

Grate the remaining ginger and mix with the oil, spring onions, wine vinegar and soy sauce and salt and pepper. Refrigerate for 1 hour. Place the chicken pieces in a serving bowl and pour over the ginger dressing. Serve with steamed rice.

Poached Chicken

Serves 4

1 chicken

1.2 1/2 pts/5 cups chicken stock or water

30 ml/2 tbsp rice wine or dry sherry

4 spring onions (scallions), chopped

1 slice ginger root

5 ml/1 tsp salt

Place the chicken in a large saucepan with all the remaining ingredients. The stock or water should come half way up the thigh. Bring to the boil, cover and simmer gently for about 1 hour until the chicken is thoroughly cooked. Drain, reserving the stock for soups.

Red-Cooked Chicken

Serves 4

1 chicken

250 ml/8 fl oz/1 cup soy sauce

Place the chicken in a pan, pour over the soy sauce and top up with water almost to cover the chicken. Bring to the boil, cover and simmer for about 1 hour until the chicken is cooked, turning occasionally.

Red-Cooked Spiced Chicken

Serves 4

2 slices ginger root

2 spring onions (scallions)

1 chicken

3 cloves star anise

½ cinnamon stick

15 ml/1 tbsp Szechuan peppercorns

75 ml/5 tbsp soy sauce

75 ml/5 tbsp rice wine or dry sherry

75 ml/5 tbsp sesame oil

15 ml/1 tbsp sugar

Place the ginger and spring onions inside the chicken cavity and place the chicken in a pan. Tie the star anise, cinnamon and peppercorns in a piece of muslin and add it to the pan. Pour over the soy sauce, wine or sherry and sesame oil. Bring to the boil, cover and simmer for about 45 minutes. Add the sugar, cover and simmer for a further 10 minutes until the chicken is cooked through.

Sesame Roast Chicken

Serves 4

50 g/2 oz sesame seeds

1 onion, finely chopped

2 cloves garlic, minced

10 ml/2 tsp salt

1 dried red chilli pepper, crushed

pinch of ground cloves

2.5 ml/½ tsp ground cardamom

2.5 ml/½ tsp ground ginger

75 ml/5 tbsp groundnut (peanut) oil

1 chicken

Mix together all the seasonings and oil and brush over the chicken. Stand it in a roasting tin and add 30 ml/2 tbsp of water to the tin. Roast in a preheated oven at 180°C/350°F/gas mark 4 for about 2 hours, basting and turning the chicken occasionally, until the chicken is golden and cooked through. Add a little more water, if necessary, to prevent burning.

Chicken in Soy Sauce

Serves 4–6

300 ml/½ pt/1¼ cups soy sauce

300 ml/½ pt/1¼ cups rice wine or dry sherry

1 onion, chopped

3 slices root ginger, minced

50 g/2 oz/¼ cup sugar

1 chicken

15 ml/1 tbsp cornflour (cornstarch)

60 ml/4 tbsp water

1 cucumber, peeled and sliced

30 ml/2 tbsp chopped fresh parsley

Mix together the soy sauce, wine or sherry, onion, ginger and sugar in a pan and bring to the boil. Add the chicken, return to the boil, cover and simmer gently for 1 hour, turning the chicken occasionally, until the chicken is cooked. Transfer the chicken to a warmed serving plate and carve. Pour out all but 250 ml/8 fl oz/1 cup of the cooking liquid and bring it back to the boil. Blend the cornflour and water to a paste, stir it into the pan and simmer, stirring, until the sauce clears and thickens. Brush a little of the sauce over the chicken and garnish the chicken with cucumber and parsley. Serve the remaining sauce separately.

Steamed Chicken

Serves 4

1 chicken

45 ml/3 tbsp rice wine or dry sherry

salt

2 slices ginger root

2 spring onions (scallions)

250 ml/8 fl oz/1 cup chicken stock

Place the chicken in an ovenproof bowl and rub with wine or sherry and salt and place the ginger and spring onions inside the cavity. Place the bowl on a rack in a steamer, cover and steam over boiling water for about 1 hour until cooked through. Serve hot or cold.

Steamed Chicken with Anise

Serves 4

250 ml/8 fl oz/1 cup soy sauce

250 ml/8 fl oz/1 cup water

15 ml/1 tbsp brown sugar

4 cloves star anise

1 chicken

Mix the soy sauce, water, sugar and anise in a saucepan and bring to the boil over a gentle heat. Place the chicken in a bowl and baste thoroughly with the mixture inside and out. Reheat the mixture and repeat. Place the chicken in an ovenproof bowl. Place the bowl on a rack in a steamer, cover and steam over boiling water for about 1 hour until cooked through.

Strange-Flavoured Chicken

Serves 4

1 chicken
5 ml/1 tsp minced ginger root
5 ml/1 tsp minced garlic
45 ml/3 tbsp thick soy sauce
5 ml/1 tsp sugar
2.5 ml/½ tsp wine vinegar
10 ml/2 tsp sesame sauce
5 ml/1 tsp freshly ground pepper
10 ml/2 tsp chilli oil
½ lettuce, shredded
15 ml/1 tbsp chopped fresh coriander

Place the chicken in a pan and fill with water to come half way up the chicken legs. Bring to the boil, cover and simmer gently for about 1 hour until the chicken is tender. Remove from the pan and drain well and soak in iced water until the meat cools completely. Drain well and chop into 5 cm/2 in pieces. Mix together all the remaining ingredients and pour over the chicken. Serve garnished with lettuce and coriander.

Crispy Chicken Chunks

Serves 4

100 g/4 oz plain (all-purpose) flour

pinch of salt

15 ml/1 tbsp water

1 egg

350 g/12 oz cooked chicken, cubed

oil for deep-frying

Mix together the flour, salt, water and egg to a fairly stiff batter, adding a little more water if necessary. Dip the chicken pieces into the batter until they are well covered. Heat the oil until very hot and deep-fry the chicken for a few minutes until crispy and golden brown.

Chicken with Green Beans

Serves 4

45 ml/3 tbsp groundnut (peanut) oil
450 g/1 lb cooked chicken, shredded
5 ml/1 tsp salt
2.5 ml/½ tsp freshly ground pepper
225 g/8 oz green beans, cut into pieces
1 stalk celery, diagonally sliced
225 g/8 oz mushrooms, sliced
250 ml/8 fl oz/1 cup chicken stock
30 ml/2 tbsp cornflour (cornstarch)
60 ml/4 tbsp water
10 ml/2 tsp soy sauce

Heat the oil and fry the chicken, salt and pepper until lightly browned. Add the beans, celery and mushrooms and mix well. Add the stock, bring to the boil, cover and simmer for 15 minutes. Mix the cornflour, water and soy sauce to a paste, stir it into the pan and simmer, stirring, until the sauce clears and thickens.

Cooked Chicken with Pineapple

Serves 4

45 ml/3 tbsp groundnut (peanut) oil
225 g/8 oz cooked chicken, diced
salt and freshly ground pepper
2 stalks celery, diagonally sliced
3 slices pineapple, cut into chunks
120 ml/4 fl oz/½ cup chicken stock
15 ml/1 tbsp soy sauce
10 ml/2 tbsp cornflour (cornstarch)
30 ml/2 tbsp water

Heat the oil and fry the chicken until lightly browned. Season with salt and pepper, add the celery and stir-fry for 2 minutes. Add the pineapple, stock and soy sauce and stir for a few minutes until heated through. Mix the cornflour and water to a paste, stir into the pan and simmer, stirring, until the sauce clears and thickens.

Chicken with Peppers and Tomatoes

Serves 4

45 ml/3 tbsp groundnut (peanut) oil
450 g/1 lb cooked chicken, sliced
10 ml/2 tsp salt
5 ml/1 tsp freshly ground pepper
1 green pepper, cut into chunks
4 large tomatoes, skinned and cut into wedges
250 ml/8 fl oz/1 cup chicken stock
30 ml/2 tbsp cornflour (cornstarch)
15 ml/1 tbsp soy sauce
120 ml/4 fl oz/½ cup water

Heat the oil and fry the chicken, salt and pepper until browned. Add the peppers and tomatoes. Pour in the stock, bring to the boil, cover and simmer for 15 minutes. Blend the cornflour, soy sauce and water to a paste, stir it into the pan and simmer, stirring, until the sauce clears and thickens.

Sesame Chicken

Serves 4

450 g/1 lb cooked chicken, cut into strips
2 slices ginger, finely chopped
1 spring onion (scallion), finely chopped
salt and freshly ground pepper
60 ml/4 tbsp rice wine or dry sherry
60 ml/4 tbsp sesame oil
10 ml/2 tsp sugar
5 ml/1 tsp wine vinegar
150 ml/¼ pt/generous ½ cup soy sauce

Arrange the chicken on a serving plate and sprinkle with ginger, spring onion, salt and pepper. Mix together the wine or sherry, sesame oil, sugar, wine vinegar and soy sauce. Pour over the chicken.

Fried Poussins

Serves 4

2 poussins, halved
45 ml/3 tbsp soy sauce
45 ml/3 tbsp rice wine or dry sherry
120 ml/4 fl oz/½ cup groundnut (peanut) oil
1 spring onion (scallion), finely chopped
30 ml/2 tbsp chicken stock
10 ml/2 tsp sugar
5 ml/1 tsp chilli oil
5 ml/1 tsp garlic paste
salt and pepper

Place the poussins in a bowl. Mix the soy sauce and wine or sherry, pour over the poussins, cover and marinate for 2 hours, basting frequently. Heat the oil and fry the poussins for about 20 minutes until cooked through. Remove them from the pan and reheat the oil. Return them to the pan and fry until golden brown. Drain off most of the oil. Mix together the remaining ingredients, add to the pan and heat through quickly. Pour over the poussins before serving.

Turkey with Mangetout

Serves 4

60 ml/4 tbsp groundnut (peanut) oil
2 spring onions (scallions), chopped
2 cloves garlic, crushed
1 slice ginger root, minced
225 g/8 oz turkey breast, cut into strips
225 g/8 oz mangetout (snow peas)
100 g/4 oz bamboo shoots, cut into strips
50 g/2 oz water chestnuts, cut into strips
45 ml/3 tbsp soy sauce
15 ml/1 tbsp rice wine or dry sherry
5 ml/1 tsp sugar
5 ml/1 tsp salt
15 ml/1 tbsp cornflour (cornstarch)

Heat 45 ml/3 tbsp of oil and fry the spring onions, garlic and ginger until lightly browned. Add the turkey and stir-fry for 5 minutes. Remove from the pan and set aside. Heat the remaining oil and stir-fry the mangetout, bamboo shoots and water chestnuts for 3 minutes. Add the soy sauce, wine or sherry, sugar and salt and return the turkey to the pan. Stir-fry for 1 minute.

Mix the cornflour with a little water, stir it into the pan and simmer, stirring, until the sauce clears and thickens.

Turkey with Peppers

Serves 4

4 dried Chinese mushrooms
30 ml/2 tbsp groundnut (peanut) oil
1 Chinese cabbage, cut into strips
350 g/12 oz smoked turkey, cut into strips
1 onion, sliced
1 red pepper, cut into strips
1 green pepper, cut into strips
120 ml/4 fl oz/½ cup chicken stock
30 ml/2 tbsp tomato purée (paste)
45 ml/3 tbsp wine vinegar
30 ml/2 tbsp soy sauce
15 ml/1 tbsp hoisin sauce
10 ml/2 tsp cornflour (cornstarch)
few drops of chilli oil

Soak the mushrooms in warm water for 30 minutes then drain. Discard the stalks and cut the caps into strips. Heat half the oil and stir-fry the cabbage for about 5 minutes or until cooked down. Remove from the pan. Add the turkey and stir-fry for 1 minute. Add the vegetables and stir-fry for 3 minutes. Mix the stock with the tomato purée, wine vinegar and sauces and add to the pan with the cabbage. Mix the cornflour with a little water, stir it into the pan and bring to the boil, stirring. Sprinkle with chilli oil and simmer for 2 minutes, stirring continuously.

Chinese Roast Turkey

Serves 8–10

1 small turkey
600 ml/1 pt/2½ cups hot water
10 ml/2 tsp allspice
500 ml/16 fl oz/2 cups soy sauce
5 ml/1 tsp sesame oil
10 ml/2 tsp salt
45 ml/3 tbsp butter

Place the turkey in a pan and pour over the hot water. Add the remaining ingredients except the butter and leave to stand for 1 hour, turning several times. Remove the turkey from the liquid and brush with butter. Place in a roasting tin, cover loosely with kitchen foil and roast in a preheated oven at 160°C/325°F/gas mark 3 for about 4 hours, basting occasionally with the soy sauce liquid. Remove the foil and allow the skin to crisp for the last 30 minutes of cooking.

Turkey with Walnuts and Mushrooms

Serves 4

450 g/1 lb turkey breast fillet
salt and pepper
juice of 1 orange
15 ml/1 tbsp plain (all-purpose) flour
12 pickled black walnuts with juice
5 ml/1 tsp cornflour (cornstarch)
15 ml/1 tbsp groundnut (peanut) oil
2 spring onions (scallions), diced
225 g/8 oz button mushrooms
45 ml/3 tbsp rice wine or dry sherry
10 ml/2 tsp soy sauce
50 g/2 oz/½ cup butter
25 g/1 oz pine kernels

Cut the turkey into 1 cm/½ in thick slices. Sprinkle with salt, pepper and orange juice and dust with flour. Drain and halve the walnuts, reserving the liquid, and mix the liquid with the cornflour. Heat the oil and stir-fry the turkey until golden brown. Add the spring onions and mushrooms and stir-fry for 2 minutes. Stir in the wine or sherry and soy sauce and simmer for 30 seconds. Add the walnuts to the cornflour mixture then stir them into the pan and bring to the boil. Add the butter in small flakes but do not allow the mixture to boil. Toast the pine kernels in a dry pan until golden. Transfer the turkey mixture to a warmed serving plate and serve garnished with pine kernels.

Duck with Bamboo Shoots

Serves 4

6 dried Chinese mushrooms
1 duck
50 g/2 oz smoked ham, cut into strips
100 g/4 oz bamboo shoots, cut into strips
2 spring onions (scallions), cut into strips
2 slices ginger root, cut into strips
5 ml/1 tsp salt

Soak the mushrooms in warm water for 30 minutes then drain. Discard the stalks and cut the caps into strips. Place all the ingredients in a heatproof bowl and stand in a pan filled with water to come two-thirds of the way up the bowl. Bring to the boil, cover and simmer for about 2 hours until the duck is cooked, topping up with boiling water as necessary.

Duck with Bean Sprouts

Serves 4

225 g/8 oz bean sprouts
45 ml/3 tbsp groundnut (peanut) oil
450 g/1 lb cooked duck meat
15 ml/1 tbsp oyster sauce
15 ml/1 tbsp rice wine or dry sherry
30 ml/2 tbsp water
2.5 ml/½ tsp salt

Blanch the bean sprouts in boiling water for 2 minutes then drain. Heat the oil, stir-fry the bean sprouts for 30 seconds. Add the duck, stir-fry until heated through. Add the remaining ingredients and stir-fry for 2 minutes to blend the flavours. Serve at once.

Braised Duck

Serves 4

4 spring onions (scallions), chopped
1 slice ginger root, minced
120 ml/4 fl oz/½ cup soy sauce
30 ml/2 tbsp rice wine or dry sherry
1 duck
120 ml/4 fl oz/½ cup groundnut (peanut) oil
600 ml/1 pt/2½ cups water
15 ml/1 tbsp brown sugar

Mix together the spring onions, ginger, soy sauce and wine or sherry and rub it over the duck inside and out. Heat the oil and fry the duck until lightly browned on all sides. Drain off the oil. Add the water and the remaining soy sauce mixture, bring to the boil then cover and simmer for 1 hour. Add the sugar then cover and simmer for a further 40 minutes until the duck is tender.

Steamed Duck with Celery

Serves 4

350 g/12 oz cooked duck, sliced
1 head celery
250 ml/8 fl oz/1 cup chicken stock
2.5 ml/½ tsp salt
5 ml/1 tsp sesame oil
1 tomato, cut into wedges

Arrange the duck on a steamer rack. Trim the celery into 7.5 cm/3 in lengths and place in a pan. Pour in the stock, season with salt and place the steamer over the pan. Bring the stock to the boil then simmer gently for about 15 minutes until the celery is tender and the duck heated through. Arrange the duck and celery on a warmed serving plate, sprinkle the celery with sesame oil and serve garnished with tomato wedges.

Duck with Ginger

Serves 4

350 g/12 oz duck breast, thinly sliced
1 egg, lightly beaten
5 ml/1 tsp soy sauce
5 ml/1 tsp cornflour (cornstarch)
5 ml/1 tsp groundnut (peanut) oil
oil for deep-frying
50 g/2 oz bamboo shoots
50 g/2 oz mangetout (snow peas)
2 slices ginger root, chopped
15 ml/1 tbsp water
2.5 ml/½ tsp sugar
2.5 ml/½ tsp rice wine or dry sherry
2.5 ml/½ tsp sesame oil

Mix the duck with the egg, soy sauce, cornflour and oil and leave to stand for 10 minutes. Heat the oil and deep-fry the duck and bamboo shoots until cooked and golden brown. Remove from the pan and drain well. Pour out all but 15 ml/1 tbsp of oil from the pan and stir-fry the duck, bamboo shoots, mangetout, ginger, water, sugar and wine or sherry for 2 minutes. Serve sprinkled with sesame oil.

Duck with Green Beans

Serves 4

1 duck

60 ml/4 tbsp groundnut (peanut) oil

2 cloves garlic, crushed

2.5 ml/½ tsp salt

1 onion, chopped

15 ml/1 tbsp grated root ginger

45 ml/3 tbsp soy sauce

120 ml/4 fl oz/½ cup rice wine or dry sherry

60 ml/4 tbsp tomato ketchup (catsup)

45 ml/3 tbsp wine vinegar

300 ml/½ pt/1¼ cups chicken stock

450 g/1 lb green beans, sliced

pinch of freshly ground pepper

5 drops chilli oil

15 ml/1 tbsp cornflour (cornstarch)

30 ml/2 tbsp water

Chop the duck into 8 or 10 pieces. Heat the oil and fry the duck until golden brown. Transfer to a bowl. Add the garlic, salt, onion, ginger, soy sauce, wine or sherry, tomato ketchup and wine vinegar. Mix, cover and marinate in the refrigerator for 3 hours.

Reheat the oil, add the duck, stock and marinade, bring to the boil, cover and simmer for 1 hour. Add the beans, cover and simmer for 15 minutes. Add the pepper and chilli oil. Mix the cornflour with the water, stir it into the pan and simmer, stirring, until the sauce thickens.

Deep-Fried Steamed Duck

Serves 4

1 duck
salt and freshly ground pepper
oil for deep-frying
hoisin sauce

Season the duck with salt and pepper and place in a heatproof bowl. Stand in a pan filled with water to come two-thirds of the way up the bowl, bring to the boil, cover and simmer for about 1½ hours until the duck is tender. Drain and leave to cool.

Heat the oil and deep-fry the duck until crispy and golden brown. Remove and drain well. Chop into bite-sized pieces and serve with hoisin sauce.

Duck with Exotic Fruits

Serves 4

4 duck breast fillets, cut into strips
2.5 ml/½ tsp five-spice powder
30 ml/2 tbsp soy sauce
15 ml/1 tbsp sesame oil
15 ml/1 tbsp groundnut (peanut) oil
3 stalks celery, diced
2 slices pineapple, diced
100 g/4 oz melon, diced
100 g/4 oz lychees, halved
130 ml/4 fl oz/½ cup chicken stock
30 ml/2 tbsp tomato purée (paste)
30 ml/2 tbsp hoisin sauce
10 ml/2 tsp wine vinegar
pinch of brown sugar

Place the duck in a bowl. Mix the five-spice powder, soy sauce and sesame oil, pour over the duck and marinate for 2 hours, stirring occasionally. Heat the oil and stir-fry the duck for 8 minutes. Remove from the pan. Add the celery and fruits and stir-fry for 5 minutes. Return the duck to the pan with the remaining ingredients, bring to the boil and simmer, stirring, for 2 minutes before serving.

Braised Duck with Chinese Leaves

Serves 4

1 duck

30 ml/2 tbsp rice wine or dry sherry

30 ml/2 tbsp hoisin sauce

15 ml/1 tbsp cornflour (cornstarch)

5 ml/1 tsp salt

5 ml/1 tsp sugar

60 ml/4 tbsp groundnut (peanut) oil

4 spring onions (scallions), chopped

2 cloves garlic, crushed

1 slice ginger root, minced

75 ml/5 tbsp soy sauce

600 ml/1 pt/2½ cups water

225 g/8 oz Chinese leaves, shredded

Cut the duck into about 6 pieces. Mix together the wine or sherry, hoisin sauce, cornflour, salt and sugar and rub over the duck. Leave to stand for 1 hour. Heat the oil and fry the spring onions, garlic and ginger for a few seconds. Add the duck and fry until lightly browned on all sides. Drain off any excess fat. Pour in the soy sauce and water, bring to the boil, cover and simmer for about 30 minutes. Add the Chinese leaves, cover again and simmer for a further 30 minutes until the duck is tender.

Drunken Duck

Serves 4

2 spring onions (scallions), chopped
2 cloves garlic, chopped
1.5 l/2½ pts/6 cups water
1 duck
450 ml/¾ pt/2 cups rice wine or dry sherry

Place the spring onions, garlic and water in a large pan and bring to the boil. Add the duck, return to the boil, cover and simmer for 45 minutes. Drain well, reserving the liquid for stock. Leave the duck to cool then refrigerate overnight. Cut the duck into pieces and place them in a large screw-top jar. Pour over the wine or sherry and chill for about 1 week before draining and serving cold.

Five-Spice Duck

Serves 4

150 ml/¼ pt/generous ½ cup rice wine or dry sherry

150 ml/¼ pt/generous ½ cup soy sauce

1 duck

10 ml/2 tsp five-spice powder

Bring the wine or sherry and soy sauce to the boil. Add the duck and simmer, turning for about 5 minutes. Remove the duck from the pan and rub the five-spice powder into the skin. Return the bird to the pan and add enough water to half cover the duck. Bring to the boil, cover and simmer for about 1½ hours until the duck is tender, turning and basting frequently. Chop the duck into 5 cm/2 in pieces and serve hot or cold.

Stir-Fried Duck with Ginger

Serves 4

1 duck

2 slices ginger root, shredded

2 spring onions (scallions), chopped

15 ml/1 tbsp cornflour (cornstarch)

30 ml/2 tbsp soy sauce

30 ml/2 tbsp rice wine or dry sherry

2.5 ml/½ tsp salt

45 ml/3 tbsp groundnut (peanut) oil

Remove the meat from the bones and cut into pieces. Mix the meat with all the remaining ingredients except the oil. Leave to stand for 1 hour. Heat the oil and stir-fry the duck with the marinade for about 15 minutes until the duck is tender.

Duck with Ham and Leeks

Serves 4

1 duck

450 g/1 lb smoked ham

2 leeks

2 slices ginger root, minced

45 ml/3 tbsp rice wine or dry sherry

45 ml/3 tbsp soy sauce

2.5 ml/½ tsp salt

Place the duck in a pan and just cover with cold water. Bring to the boil, cover and simmer for about 20 minutes. Drain and reserve 450 ml/¾ pts/2 cups of stock. Let the duck cool slightly then cut the meat from the bones and cut it into 5 cm/2 in squares. Cut the ham into similar pieces. Cut off long pieces of leek and roll a slice of duck and ham inside the leaf and tie with string. Place in a heatproof bowl. Add the ginger, wine or sherry, soy sauce and salt to the reserved stock and pour it over the duck rolls. Place the bowl in a pan filled with water to come two-thirds of the way up the sides of the bowl. Bring to the boil, cover and simmer for about 1 hour until the duck is tender.

Honey-Roast Duck

Serves 4

1 duck

salt

3 cloves garlic, crushed

3 spring onions (scallions), minced

45 ml/3 tbsp soy sauce

45 ml/3 tbsp rice wine or dry sherry

45 ml/3 tbsp honey

200 ml/7 fl oz/scant 1 cup boiling water

Pat the duck dry and rub with salt inside and out. Mix the garlic, spring onions, soy sauce and wine or sherry then divide the mixture in half. Mix the honey into one half and rub over the duck then leave it to dry. Add the water to the remaining honey mixture. Pour the soy sauce mixture into the cavity of the duck and stand it on a rack in a roasting tin with a little water in the bottom. Roast in a preheated oven at 180°C/350°F/gas mark 4 for about 2 hours until the duck is tender, basting throughout cooking with the remaining honey mixture.

Moist Roast Duck

Serves 4

6 spring onions (scallions), chopped

2 slices ginger root, minced

1 duck

2.5 ml/½ tsp ground anise

15 ml/1 tbsp sugar

45 ml/3 tbsp rice wine or dry sherry

60 ml/4 tbsp soy sauce

250 ml/8 fl oz/1 cup water

Place half the spring onions and ginger in a large heavy-based pan. Place the remainder in the cavity of the duck and add it to the pan. Add all the remaining ingredients except the hoisin sauce, bring to the boil, cover and simmer for about 1½ hours, turning occasionally. Remove the duck from the pan and leave it to dry for about 4 hours.

Place the duck on a rack in a roasting tin filled with a little cold water. Roast in a preheated oven at 230°C/450°F/gas mark 8 for 15 minutes then turn it over and roast for a further 10 minutes until crispy. Meanwhile, reheat the reserved liquid and pour over the duck to serve.

Stir-Fried Duck with Mushrooms

Serves 4

1 duck

75 ml/5 tbsp groundnut (peanut) oil

45 ml/3 tbsp rice wine or dry sherry

15 ml/1 tbsp soy sauce

15 ml/1 tbsp sugar

5 ml/1 tsp salt

pinch of pepper

2 cloves garlic, crushed

225 g/8 oz mushrooms, halved

600 ml/1 pt/2½ cups chicken stock

15 ml/1 tbsp cornflour (cornstarch)

30 ml/2 tbsp water

5 ml/1 tsp sesame oil

Chop the duck into 5 cm/2 in pieces. Heat 45 ml/3 tbsp of oil and fry the duck until lightly browned on all sides. Add the wine or sherry, soy sauce, sugar, salt and pepper and stir-fry for 4 minutes. Remove from the pan. Heat the remaining oil and fry the garlic until lightly browned. Add the mushrooms and stir until coated in oil then return the duck mixture to the pan and add the stock. Bring to the boil, cover and simmer for about 1 hour until the duck is tender. Mix the cornflour and water to a paste then stir it into the mixture and simmer, stirring, until the sauce thickens. Sprinkle with sesame oil and serve.

Duck with Two Mushrooms

Serves 4

6 dried Chinese mushrooms
1 duck
750 ml/1¼ pts/3 cups chicken stock
45 ml/3 tbsp rice wine or dry sherry
5 ml/1 tsp salt
100 g/4 oz bamboo shoots, cut into strips
100 g/4 oz button mushrooms

Soak the mushrooms in warm water for 30 minutes then drain. Discard the stalks and halve the caps. Place the duck in a large heatproof bowl with the stock, wine or sherry and salt and stand in a pan filled with water to come two-thirds up the sides of the bowl. Bring to the boil, cover and simmer for about 2 hours until the duck is tender. Remove from the pan and cut the meat from the bone. Transfer the cooking liquid to a separate pan. Arrange the bamboo shoots and both types of mushrooms in the bottom of the steamer bowl, replace the duck meat, cover and steam for a further 30 minutes. Bring the cooking liquid to the boil and pour over the duck to serve.

Braised Duck with Onions

Serves 4

4 dried Chinese mushrooms
1 duck
90 ml/6 tbsp soy sauce
60 ml/4 tbsp groundnut (peanut) oil
1 spring onion (scallion), chopped
1 slice ginger root, minced
45 ml/3 tbsp rice wine or dry sherry
450 g/1 lb onions, sliced
100 g/4 oz bamboo shoots, sliced
15 ml/1 tbsp brown sugar
15 ml/1 tbsp cornflour (cornstarch)
45 ml/3 tbsp water

Soak the mushrooms in warm water for 30 minutes then drain. Discard the stalks and slice the caps. Rub 15 ml/1 tbsp of soy sauce into the duck. Reserve 15 ml/1 tbsp of oil, heat the remaining oil and fry the spring onion and ginger until lightly browned. Add the duck and fry until lightly browned on all sides. Pour off any excess fat. Add the wine or sherry, remaining soy sauce to the pan and just enough water almost to cover the duck.

Bring to the boil, cover and simmer for 1 hour, turning occasionally.

Heat the reserved oil and fry the onions until softened. Remove from the heat and stir in the bamboo shoots and mushrooms then add them to the duck, cover and simmer for a further 30 minutes until the duck is tender. Remove the duck from the pan, cut into serving pieces and arrange on a warmed serving plate. Bring the liquids in the pan to the boil, add the sugar and cornflour and simmer, stirring, until the mixture boils and thickens. Pour over the duck to serve.

Duck with Orange

Serves 4

1 duck

3 spring onions (scallions), cut into chunks

2 slices ginger root, cut into strips

1 slice orange rind

salt and freshly ground pepper

Place the duck in a large pan, just cover with water and bring to the boil. Add the spring onions, ginger and orange rind, cover and simmer for about 1½ hours until the duck is tender. Season with salt and pepper, drain and serve.

Orange-Roast Duck

Serves 4

1 duck

2 cloves garlic, halved

45 ml/3 tbsp groundnut (peanut) oil

1 onion

1 orange

120 ml/4 fl oz/½ cup rice wine or dry sherry

2 slices ginger root, minced

5 ml/1 tsp salt

Rub the garlic over the duck inside and out then brush it with oil. Pierce the peeled onion with a fork, place it and the unpeeled orange inside the duck cavity and seal with a skewer. Stand the duck on a rack over a roasting tin filled with a little hot water and roast in a preheated oven at 160°C/325°F/gas mark 3 for about 2 hours. Discard the liquids and return the duck to the roasting tin. Pour over the wine or sherry and sprinkle with the ginger and salt. Return to the oven for a further 30 minutes. Discard the onion and orange and cut the duck into serving pieces. Pour the pan juices over the duck to serve.

Duck with Pears and Chestnuts

Serves 4

225 g/8 oz chestnuts, shelled

1 duck

45 ml/3 tbsp groundnut (peanut) oil

250 ml/8 fl oz/1 cup chicken stock

45 ml/3 tbsp soy sauce

15 ml/1 tbsp rice wine or dry sherry

5 ml/1 tsp salt

1 slice ginger root, minced

1 large pear, peeled and thickly sliced

15 ml/1 tbsp sugar

Boil the chestnuts for 15 minutes then drain. Chop the duck into 5 cm/2 in pieces. Heat the oil and fry the duck until lightly browned on all sides. Drain off any excess oil then add the stock, soy sauce, wine or sherry, salt and ginger. Bring to the boil, cover and simmer for 25 minutes, stirring occasionally. Add the chestnuts, cover and simmer for a further 15 minutes. Sprinkle the pear with sugar, add to the pan and simmer for about 5 minutes until heated through.

Peking Duck

Serves 6

1 duck

250 ml/8 fl oz/1 cup water

120 ml/4 fl oz/½ cup honey

120 ml/4 fl oz/½ cup sesame oil

For the pancakes:

250 ml/8 fl oz/1 cup water

225 g/8 oz/2 cups plain (all-purpose) flour

groundnut (peanut) oil for frying

For the dips:

120 ml/4 fl oz/½ cup hoisin sauce

30 ml/2 tbsp brown sugar

30 ml/2 tbsp soy sauce

5 ml/1 tsp sesame oil

6 spring onions (scallions), sliced lengthways

1 cucumber, cut into strips

The duck should be whole with the skin intact. Tie the neck tightly with string and sew up or skewer the bottom opening. Cut a small slit in the side of the neck, insert a straw and blow air under the skin until it is inflated. Suspend the duck over a basin and leave to hang for 1 hour.

Bring a pan of water to the boil, insert the duck and boil for 1 minute then remove and dry well. Bring the water to the boil and stir in the honey. Rub the mixture over the duck skin until it is saturated. Hang the duck over a basin in a cool, airy place for about 8 hours until the skin is hard.

Suspend the duck or place on a rack over a roasting tin and roast in a preheated oven at 180°C/350°F/gas mark 4 for about 1½ hours, basting regularly with sesame oil.

To make the pancakes, boil the water then gradually add the flour. Knead lightly until the dough is soft, cover with a damp cloth and leave to stand for 15 minutes. Roll out on a floured surface and shape into a long cylinder. Cut into 2.5 cm/1 in slices then flatten until about 5 mm/¼ in thick and brush the tops with oil. Stack in pairs with the oiled surfaces touching and dust the outsides lightly with flour. Roll out the pairs to about 10 cm/4 in across and cook in pairs for about 1 minute on each side until lightly browned. Separate and stack until ready to serve.

Prepare the dips by mixing half the hoisin sauce with the sugar and mixing the remaining hoisin sauce with the soy sauce and sesame oil.

Remove the duck from the oven, cut off the skin and cut it into squares, and cube the meat. Arrange on separate plates and serve with the pancakes, dips and accompaniments.

Braised Duck with Pineapple

Serves 4

1 duck
400 g/14 oz canned pineapple chunks in syrup
45 ml/3 tbsp soy sauce
5 ml/1 tsp salt
pinch of freshly ground pepper

Place the duck in a heavy-based pan, just cover with water, bring to the boil then cover and simmer for 1 hour. Drain the pineapple syrup into the pan with the soy sauce, salt and pepper, cover and simmer for a further 30 minutes. Add the pineapple pieces and simmer for a further 15 minutes until the duck is tender.

Stir-Fried Duck with Pineapple

Serves 4

1 duck
45 ml/3 tbsp cornflour (cornstarch)
45 ml/3 tbsp soy sauce
225 g/8 oz canned pineapple in syrup
45 ml/3 tbsp groundnut (peanut) oil
2 slices ginger root, cut into strips
15 ml/1 tbsp rice wine or dry sherry
5 ml/1 tsp salt

Cut the meat from the bone and cut it into pieces. Mix the soy sauce with 30 ml/2 tbsp of cornflour and mix into the duck until well coated. Leave to stand for 1 hour, stirring occasionally. Crush the pineapple and syrup and heat gently in a pan. Mix the remaining cornflour with a little water, stir into the pan and simmer, stirring, until the sauce thickens. Keep warm. Heat the oil and fry the ginger until lightly browned then discard the ginger. Add the duck and stir-fry until lightly browned on all sides. Add the wine or sherry and salt and stir-fry for a further few minutes until the duck is cooked. Arrange the duck on a warmed serving plate, pour over the sauce and serve at once.

Pineapple and Ginger Duck

Serves 4

1 duck
100 g/4 oz preserved ginger in syrup
200 g/7 oz canned pineapple chunks in syrup
5 ml/1 tsp salt
15 ml/1 tbsp cornflour (cornstarch)
30 ml/2 tbsp water

Place the duck in a heatproof bowl and stand it in a pan filled with water to come two-thirds of the way up the sides of the bowl. Bring to the boil, cover and simmer for about 2 hours until the duck is tender. Remove the duck and leave to cool slightly. Remove the skin and bone and cut the duck into pieces. Arrange on a serving plate and keep them warm.

Drain the syrup from the ginger and pineapple into a pan, add the salt, cornflour and water. Bring to the boil, stirring and simmer for a few minutes, stirring, until the sauce clears and thickens. Add the ginger and pineapple, stir through then pour over the duck to serve.

Duck with Pineapple and Lychees

Serves 4

4 duck breasts
15 ml/1 tbsp soy sauce
1 clove star anise
1 slice ginger root
groundnut (peanut) oil for deep-frying
90 ml/6 tbsp wine vinegar
100 g/4 oz/½ cup brown sugar
250 ml/8 fl oz/½ cup chicken stock
15 ml/1 tbsp tomato ketchup (catsup)
200 g/7 oz canned pineapple chunks in syrup
15 ml/1 tbsp cornflour (cornstarch)
6 canned lychees
6 maraschino cherries

Place the ducks, soy sauce, anise and ginger in a saucepan and just cover with cold water. Bring to the boil, skim, then cover and simmer for about 45 minutes until the duck is cooked. Drain and pat dry. Deep-fry in hot oil until crispy.

Meanwhile, mix the wine vinegar, sugar, stock, tomato ketchup and 30 ml/2 tbsp of the pineapple syrup in a pan, bring to the boil and simmer for about 5 minutes until thick. Stir in the fruit and heat through before pouring over the duck to serve.

Duck with Pork and Chestnuts

Serves 4

6 dried Chinese mushrooms
1 duck
225 g/8 oz chestnuts, shelled
225 g/8 oz lean pork, cubed
3 spring onions (scallions), chopped
1 slice ginger root, minced
250 ml/8 fl oz/1 cup soy sauce
900 ml/1½ pts/3¾ cups water

Soak the mushrooms in warm water for 30 minutes then drain. Discard the stalks and slice the caps. Place in a large pan with all the remaining ingredients, bring to the boil, cover and simmer for about 1½ hours until the duck is cooked.

Duck with Potatoes

Serves 4

75 ml/5 tbsp groundnut (peanut) oil

1 duck

3 cloves garlic, crushed

30 ml/2 tbsp black bean sauce

10 ml/2 tsp salt

1.2 l/2 pts/5 cups water

2 leeks, thickly sliced

15 ml/1 tbsp sugar

45 ml/3 tbsp soy sauce

60 ml/4 tbsp rice wine or dry sherry

1 clove star anise

900 g/2 lb potatoes, thickly sliced

½ head Chinese leaves

15 ml/1 tbsp cornflour (cornstarch)

30 ml/2 tbsp water

sprigs flat-leaf parsley

Heat 60 ml/4 tbsp of oil and fry the duck until browned on all sides. Tie or sew up the neck end and stand the duck, neck down, in a deep bowl. Heat the remaining oil and fry the garlic until lightly browned. Add the black bean sauce and salt and fry for 1 minute. Add the water, leeks, sugar, soy sauce, wine or sherry and star anise and bring to the boil. Pour 120 ml/8 fl oz/1 cup of the mixture into the duck cavity and tie or sew up to secure. Bring the remaining mixture in the pan to the boil. Add the duck and potatoes, cover and simmer for 40 minutes, turning the duck once. Arrange the Chinese leaves on a serving plate. Remove the duck from the pan, chop into 5 cm/2 in pieces and arrange on the serving plate with the potatoes. Mix the cornflour to a paste with the water, stir it into the pan and simmer, stirring, until the sauce thickens. Pour over the duck and serve garnished with parsley.

Red-Cooked Duck

Serves 4

1 duck

4 spring onions (scallions), cut into chunks

2 slices ginger root, cut into strips

90 ml/6 tbsp soy sauce

45 ml/3 tbsp rice wine or dry sherry

10 ml/2 tsp salt

10 ml/2 tsp sugar

Place the duck in a heavy pan, just cover with water and bring to the boil. Add the spring onions, ginger, wine or sherry and salt, cover and simmer for about 1 hour. Add the sugar and simmer for a further 45 minutes until the duck is tender. Slice the duck on to a serving plate and serve hot or cold, with or without the sauce.

Rice Wine Roast Duck

Serves 4

1 duck

500 ml/14 fl oz/1¾ cups rice wine or dry sherry

5 ml/1 tsp salt

45 ml/3 tbsp soy sauce

Place the duck in a heavy-based pan with the sherry and salt, bring to the boil, cover and simmer for 20 minutes. Drain the duck, reserving the liquid, and rub it with soy sauce. Place on a rack in a roasting tin filled with a little hot water and roast in a preheated oven at 180°C/350°F/gas mark 4 for about 1 hour, basting regularly with the reserved wine liquid.

Steamed Duck with Rice Wine

Serves 4

1 duck

4 spring onions (scallions), halved

1 slice ginger root, chopped

250 ml/8 fl oz/1 cup rice wine or dry sherry

30 ml/2 tbsp soy sauce

pinch of salt

Blanch the duck in boiling water for 5 minutes then drain. Place in a heatproof bowl with the remaining ingredients. Stand the bowl in a pan filled with water to come two-thirds of the way up the sides of the bowl. Bring to the boil, cover and simmer for about 2 hours until the duck is tender. Discard the spring onions and ginger before serving.

Savoury Duck

Serves 4

45 ml/3 tbsp groundnut (peanut) oil

4 duck breasts

3 spring onions (scallions), sliced

2 cloves garlic, crushed

1 slice ginger root, chopped

250 ml/8 fl oz/1 cup soy sauce

30 ml/2 tbsp rice wine or dry sherry

30 ml/2 tbsp brown sugar

5 ml/1 tsp salt

450 ml/¾ pt/2 cups water

15 ml/1 tbsp cornflour (cornstarch)

Heat the oil and fry the duck breasts until golden brown. Add the spring onions, garlic and ginger and fry for 2 minutes. Add the soy sauce, wine or sherry, sugar and salt and mix well. Add the water, bring to the boil, cover and simmer for about 1½ hours until the meat is very tender. Mix the cornflour with a little water then stir it into the pan and simmer, stirring, until the sauce thickens.

Savoury Duck with Green Beans

Serves 4

45 ml/3 tbsp groundnut (peanut) oil
4 duck breasts
3 spring onions (scallions), sliced
2 cloves garlic, crushed
1 slice ginger root, chopped
250 ml/8 fl oz/1 cup soy sauce
30 ml/2 tbsp rice wine or dry sherry
30 ml/2 tbsp brown sugar
5 ml/1 tsp salt
450 ml/¾ pt/2 cups water
225 g/8 oz green beans
15 ml/1 tbsp cornflour (cornstarch)

Heat the oil and fry the duck breasts until golden brown. Add the spring onions, garlic and ginger and fry for 2 minutes. Add the soy sauce, wine or sherry, sugar and salt and mix well. Add the water, bring to the boil, cover and simmer for about 45 minutes. Add the beans, cover and simmer for a further 20 minutes. Mix the cornflour with a little water then stir it into the pan and simmer, stirring, until the sauce thickens.

Slow-Cooked Duck

Serves 4

1 duck

50 g/2 oz/½ cup cornflour (cornstarch)

oil for deep-frying

2 cloves garlic, crushed

30 ml/2 tbsp rice wine or dry sherry

30 ml/2 tbsp soy sauce

5 ml/1 tsp grated ginger root

750 ml/1¼ pts/3 cups chicken stock

4 dried Chinese mushrooms

225 g/8 oz bamboo shoots, sliced

225 g/8 oz water chestnuts, sliced

10 ml/2 tsp sugar

pinch of pepper

5 spring onions (scallions), sliced

Cut the duck into serving-size pieces. Reserve 30 ml/2 tbsp of cornflour and coat the duck in the remaining cornflour. Dust off the excess. Heat the oil and fry the garlic and duck until lightly browned. Remove from the pan and drain on kitchen paper. Place the duck in a large pan. Mix together the wine or sherry, 15 ml/1 tbsp of soy sauce and the ginger. Add to the pan and cook over a high heat for 2 minutes. Add half the stock, bring to the boil, cover and simmer for about 1 hour until the duck is tender.

Meanwhile, soak the mushrooms in warm water for 30 minutes then drain. Discard the stalks and slice the caps. Add the mushrooms, bamboo shoots and water chestnuts to the duck and cook, stirring frequently, for 5 minutes. Skim off any fat from the liquid. Blend the remaining stock, cornflour and soy sauce with the sugar and pepper and stir into the pan. Bring to the boil, stirring, then simmer for about 5 minutes until the sauce thickens. Transfer to a warmed serving bowl and serve garnished with spring onions.

Stir-Fried Duck

Serves 4

1 egg white, lightly beaten

20 ml/1½ tbsp cornflour (cornstarch)

salt

450 g/1 lb duck breasts, thinly sliced

45 ml/3 tbsp groundnut (peanut) oil

2 spring onions (scallions), cut into strips

1 green pepper, cut into strips

5 ml/1 tsp rice wine or dry sherry

75 ml/5 tbsp chicken stock

2.5 ml/½ tsp sugar

Beat the egg white with 15 ml/1 tbsp of cornflour and a pinch of salt. Add the sliced duck and mix until the duck is coated. Heat the oil and fry the duck until cooked through and golden. Remove the duck from the pan and drain off all but 30 ml/2 tbsp of the oil. Add the spring onions and pepper and stir-fry for 3 minutes. Add the wine or sherry, stock and sugar and bring to the boil. Mix the remaining cornflour with a little water, stir it into the sauce and simmer, stirring, until the sauce thickens. Stir in the duck, heat through and serve.

Duck with Sweet Potatoes

Serves 4

1 duck

250 ml/8 fl oz/1 cup groundnut (peanut) oil

225 g/8 oz sweet potatoes, peeled and cubed

2 cloves garlic, crushed

1 slice ginger root, minced

2.5 ml/½ tsp cinnamon

2.5 ml/½ tsp ground cloves

pinch of ground anise

5 ml/1 tsp sugar

15 ml/1 tbsp soy sauce

250 ml/8 fl oz/1 cup chicken stock

15 ml/1 tbsp cornflour (cornstarch)

30 ml/2 tbsp water

Chop the duck into 5 cm/2 in pieces. Heat the oil and deep-fry the potatoes until golden brown. Remove them from the pan and drain off all but 30 ml/2 tbsp of oil. Add the garlic and ginger and stir-fry for 30 seconds. Add the duck and fry until lightly browned on all sides. Add the spices, sugar, soy sauce and stock and bring to the boil. Add the potatoes, cover and simmer for about 20 minutes until the duck is tender. Blend the cornflour to a paste with the water then stir it into the pan and simmer, stirring, until the sauce thickens.

Sweet and Sour Duck

Serves 4

1 duck

1.2 l/2 pts/5 cups chicken stock

2 onions

2 carrots

2 cloves garlic, sliced

15 ml/1 tbsp pickling spice

10 ml/2 tsp salt

10 ml/2 tsp groundnut (peanut) oil

6 spring onions (scallions), chopped

1 mango, peeled and cubed

12 lychees, halved

15 ml/1 tbsp cornflour (cornstarch)

15 ml/1 tbsp wine vinegar

10 ml/2 tsp tomato purée (paste)

15 ml/1 tbsp soy sauce

5 ml/1 tsp five-spice powder

300 ml/½ pt/1¼ cups chicken stock

Arrange the duck in a steam basket over a pan containing the stock, onions, carrots, garlic, pickling spice and salt. Cover and steam for 2½ hours. Cool the duck, cover and chill for 6 hours.

Remove the meat from the bones and cut it into cubes. Heat the oil and fry the duck and spring onions until crisp. Stir in the remaining ingredients, bring to the boil and simmer for 2 minutes, stirring, until the sauce thickens.

Tangerine Duck

Serves 4

1 duck
60 ml/4 tbsp groundnut (peanut) oil
1 piece dried tangerine peel
900 ml/1½ pts/3¾ cups chicken stock
5 ml/1 tsp salt

Hang the duck to dry for 2 hours. Heat half the oil and fry the duck until lightly browned. Transfer to a large heatproof bowl. Heat the remaining oil and fry the tangerine peel for 2 minutes then place it inside the duck. Pour the stock over the duck and season with salt. Place the bowl on a rack in a steamer, cover and steam for about 2 hours until the duck is tender.

Duck with Vegetables

Serves 4

1 large duck, chopped into 16 pieces
salt
300 ml/½ pt/1¼ cups water
300 ml/½ pt/1¼ cups dry white wine
120 ml/4 fl oz/½ cup wine vinegar
45 ml/3 tbsp soy sauce
30 ml/2 tbsp plum sauce
30 ml/2 tbsp hoisin sauce
5 ml/1 tsp five-spice powder
6 spring onions (scallions), chopped
2 carrots, chopped
5 cm/2 in white radish, chopped
50 g/2 oz Chinese cabbage, diced
freshly ground pepper
5 ml/1 tsp sugar

Put the duck pieces in a bowl, sprinkle with salt and add the water and wine. Add the wine vinegar, soy sauce, plum sauce, hoisin sauce and five-spice powder, bring to the boil, cover and simmer for about 1 hour. Add the vegetables to the pan, remove the lid and simmer for a further 10 minutes. Season with salt, pepper and sugar then leave to cool. Cover and refrigerate overnight. Skim off any fat then reheat the duck in the sauce for 20 minutes.

Stir-Fried Duck with Vegetables

Serves 4

4 dried Chinese mushrooms
1 duck
10 ml/2 tsp cornflour (cornstarch)
15 ml/1 tbsp soy sauce
45 ml/3 tbsp groundnut (peanut) oil
100 g/4 oz bamboo shoots, cut into strips
50 g/2 oz water chestnuts, cut into strips
120 ml/4 fl oz/½ cup chicken stock
15 ml/1 tbsp rice wine or dry sherry
5 ml/1 tsp salt

Soak the mushrooms in warm water for 30 minutes then drain. Discard the stalks and dice the caps. Remove the meat from the bones and cut into pieces. Mix the cornflour and soy sauce, add to the duck meat and leave to stand for 1 hour. Heat the oil and fry the duck until lightly browned on all sides. Remove from the pan. Add the mushrooms, bamboo shoots and water chestnuts to the pan and stir-fry for 3 minutes. Add the stock, wine or sherry and salt, bring to the boil and simmer for 3 minutes. Return the duck to the pan, cover and simmer for a further 10 minutes until the duck is tender.

White-Cooked Duck

Serves 4

1 slice ginger root, chopped
250 ml/8 fl oz/1 cup rice wine or dry sherry
salt and freshly ground pepper
1 duck
3 spring onions (scallions), chopped
5 ml/1 tsp salt
100 g/4 oz bamboo shoots, sliced
100 g/4 oz smoked ham, sliced

Mix the ginger, 15 ml/1 tbsp wine or sherry, a little salt and pepper. Rub over the duck and leave to stand for 1 hour. Place the bird in a heavy-based pan with the marinade and add the spring onions and salt. Add enough cold water just to cover the duck, bring to the boil, cover and simmer for about 2 hours until the duck is tender. Add the bamboo shoots and ham and simmer for a further 10 minutes.

Duck with Wine

Serves 4

1 duck

15 ml/1 tbsp yellow bean sauce

1 onion, sliced

1 bottle dry white wine

Rub the duck inside and out with the yellow bean sauce. Place the onion inside the cavity. Bring the wine to the boil in a large pan, add the duck, return to the boil, cover and simmer as gently as possible for about 3 hours until the duck is tender. Drain and slice to serve.

Wine-Vapour Duck

Serves 4

1 duck
celery salt
200 ml/7 fl oz/scant 1 cup rice wine or dry sherry
30 ml/2 tbsp chopped fresh parsley

Rub the duck with celery salt inside and out then place it in a deep ovenproof dish. Place an ovenproof cup containing the wine into the cavity of the duck. Place the dish on a rack in a steamer, cover and steam over boiling water for about 2 hours until the duck is tender.

Fried Pheasant

Serves 4

900 g/2 lb pheasant
30 ml/2 tbsp soy sauce
4 eggs, beaten
120 ml/4 fl oz/½ cup groundnut (peanut) oil

Bone the pheasant and slice the meat. Mix with the soy sauce and leave to stand for 30 minutes. Drain the pheasant then dip it in the eggs. Heat the oil and fry the pheasant quickly until golden brown. Drain well before serving.

Pheasant with Almonds

Serves 4

45 ml/3 tbsp groundnut (peanut) oil
2 spring onions (scallions), chopped
1 slice ginger root, minced
225 g/8 oz pheasant, very thinly sliced
50 g/2 oz ham, shredded
30 ml/2 tbsp soy sauce
30 ml/2 tbsp rice wine or dry sherry
5 ml/1 tsp sugar
5 ml/1 tsp freshly ground pepper
2.5 ml/½ tsp salt
100 g/4 oz/1 cup flaked almonds

Heat the oil and fry the spring onions and ginger until lightly browned. Add the pheasant and ham and stir-fry for 5 minutes until almost cooked. Add the soy sauce, wine or sherry, sugar, pepper and salt and stir-fry for 2 minutes. Add the almonds and stir-fry for 1 minute until the ingredients are thoroughly blended.

Venison with Dried Mushrooms

Serves 4

8 dried Chinese mushrooms
450 g/1 lb venison fillet, cut into strips
15 ml/1 tbsp juniper berries, ground
15 ml/1 tbsp sesame oil
30 ml/2 tbsp soy sauce
30 ml/2 tbsp hoisin sauce
5 ml/1 tsp five-spice powder
30 ml/2 tbsp groundnut (peanut) oil
6 spring onions (scallions), chopped
30 ml/2 tbsp honey
30 ml/2 tbsp wine vinegar

Soak the mushrooms in warm water for 30 minutes then drain. Discard the stalks and slice the caps. Place the venison in a bowl. Mix the juniper berries, sesame oil, soy sauce, hoisin sauce and five-spice powder, pour over the venison and marinate for at least 3 hours, stirring occasionally. Heat the oil and stir-fry the meat for 8 minutes until cooked. Remove from the pan. Add the spring onions and mushrooms to the pan and stir-fry for 3 minutes. Return the meat to the pan with the honey and wine vinegar and heat through, stirring.

Salted Eggs

Makes 6

1.2 l/2 pts/5 cups water

100 g/4 oz rock salt

6 duck eggs

Bring the water to the boil with the salt and stir until the salt has dissolved. Leave to cool. Pour the salt water into a large jar, add the eggs, cover and leave to stand for 1 month. Hard-boil the eggs before steaming with rice.

Soy Eggs

Serves 4

4 eggs

120 ml/4 fl oz/½ cup soy sauce

120 ml/4 fl oz/½ cup water

50 g/2 oz/¼ cup brown sugar

½ head lettuce, shredded

2 tomatoes, sliced

Place the eggs in a saucepan, cover with cold water, bring to the boil and boil for 10 minutes. Drain and cool under running water. Return the eggs to the pan and add the soy sauce, water and sugar. Bring to the boil, cover and simmer for 1 hour. Arrange the lettuce on a serving plate. Quarter the eggs and place on top of the lettuce. Serve garnished with tomatoes.

Tea Eggs

Serves 4–6

6 eggs

10 ml/2 tsp salt

3 China tea bags

45 ml/3 tbsp soy sauce

1 clove star anise, broken apart

Place the eggs in a pan, cover with cold water then bring to a slow boil and simmer for 15 minutes. Remove from the heat and place the eggs in cold water until cool. Leave to stand for 5 minutes. Remove the eggs from the pan and gently crack the shells but do not remove them. Return the eggs to the pan and cover with cold water. Add the remaining ingredients, bring to the boil then simmer for 1½ hours. Cool and remove the shell.

Egg Custard

Serves 4

4 eggs, beaten

375 ml/13 fl oz/1½ cups chicken stock

2.5 ml/½ tsp salt

1 spring onion (scallion), minced

100 g/4 oz peeled prawns, roughly chopped

15 ml/1 tbsp soy sauce

15 ml/1 tbsp groundnut (peanut) oil

Mix all the ingredients except the oil in a deep bowl and stand the bowl in a roasting tin filled with 2.5 cm/1 in of water. Cover and steam for 15 minutes. Heat the oil and pour it over the custard. Cover and steam for a further 15 minutes.

Steamed Eggs

Serves 4

250 ml/8 fl oz/1 cup chicken stock

4 eggs, lightly beaten

15 ml/1 tbsp rice wine or dry sherry

5 ml/1 tsp groundnut (peanut) oil

2.5 ml/½ tsp salt

2.5 ml/½ tsp sugar

2 spring onions (scallions), chopped

15 ml/1 tbsp soy sauce

Beat the eggs lightly with the wine or sherry, oil, salt, sugar and spring onions. Warm the stock then slowly stir it into the egg mixture and pour into a shallow ovenproof dish. Place the dish on a rack in a steamer, cover and steam for about 30 minutes over gently simmering water until the mixture is the consistency of thick custard. Sprinkle with soy sauce before serving.

www.ingramcontent.com/pod-product-compliance
Lightning Source LLC
Chambersburg PA
CBHW071819080526
44589CB00012B/856